Collective Biographies

CONFEDERATE GENERALS OF THE CIVIL WAR

Carl R. Green
and
William R. Sanford

Enslow Publishers, Inc.

44 Fadem Road	PO Box 38
Box 699	Aldershot
Springfield, NJ 07081	Hants GU12 6BP
USA	UK

Library of Congress Cataloging-in-Publication Data

Green, Carl R.
    Confederate generals of the Civil War / Carl R. Green and
William R. Sanford.
        p. cm. — (Collective biographies)
    Includes bibliographical references and index.
    ISBN 0-7660-1029-5
    Summary: Profiles ten Confederate Generals: Nathan Bedford Forrest; William
Joseph Hardee; Ambrose Powell Hill; John Bell Hood; Thomas "Stonewall"
Jackson; Joseph Eggleston Johnston; Robert E. Lee; James Longstreet; George
Edward Pickett; James Ewell Brown "Jeb" Stuart.
    1. Generals—Confederate States of America—Biography—Juvenile
literature. 2. Confederate States of America. Army—Biography—
Juvenile literature. 3. United States—History—Civil War,
1861–1865—Biography—Juvenile literature. I. Sanford, William R.
II. Title. III. Series.
E467.S27 1998
973.7'42'0922—dc21
    [B]   97–28014
                                                        CIP
                                                         AC

Printed in the United States of America

10 9 8 7 6 5 4 3 2 1

Illustration Credits: Digital Stock Historical pp. 18, 28, 34, 48, 53, 66, 73,
80, 90, 94; Enslow Publishers, Inc. p. 8; National Archives pp. 12, 22, 30,
40, 58, 76, 84; William R. Sanford and Carl R. Green pp. 44, 62, 100.

Cover Illustration: Library of Congress

Contents

Introduction 4

Northern vs. Southern
States: a Comparison 7

Map of the Civil War 8

Time Line: Major Events
of the Civil War 9

1 Nathan Bedford Forrest 12

2 William Joseph Hardee 21

3 Ambrose Powell Hill 30

4 John Bell Hood 39

5 Thomas "Stonewall" Jackson 48

6 Joe Johnston 57

7 Robert E. Lee 66

8 James Longstreet 75

9 George Edward Pickett 84

10 "Jeb" Stuart 93

Military Units 102

The Officer Corps 103

Glossary 104

Chapter Notes 107

Index 111

Introduction

On April 12, 1861, Southern guns opened fire on Fort Sumter, South Carolina. The deadly barrage set off the American Civil War. Generals of the North and South led troops through four years of fierce, bloody battles. By the time the guns fell silent, 620,000 Americans had died in a struggle to determine the nation's future.

In the years before the war the United States had grown prosperous, productive—and deeply divided. Southern states threatened to leave the Union if their rights under the Constitution were violated. Their leaders cherished a rural way of life that used African-American slaves to grow cotton and tobacco on large plantations. In the North farmers grew corn and wheat on small family plots. Northern cities bustled with commerce. On street corners abolitionists preached the evils of slavery. The South felt besieged and talked of secession. The North vowed to fight any attempt to divide the nation.

When war came, Southerners boasted that each of their soldiers was equal to five northern soldiers. Given the North's immense resources, the South's confidence was based on faith, not facts (see the comparison that follows this introduction).

General-in-Chief Winfield Scott designed the Union's Anaconda Plan. As the name implied, its aim was to squeeze the South into submission. At sea warships blockaded Southern ports and tried to cut off trade. On land Union forces moved to take control of the Mississippi River in an attempt to split the Southern states. That task finished, the Federals stormed into Georgia. To complete the encirclement, the Army of the Potomac set its sights on the Confederate capital at Richmond, Virginia.

The South countered with the Davis Plan, a mixture of diplomacy and armed force. On one front, Southern envoys sailed to Europe to bargain for diplomatic recognition as well as economic and military aid. At home, outnumbered Southern armies prepared to fight a defensive war. Win a few major battles or inflict heavy losses on Union forces, Southern leaders promised, and the North will give up the struggle.

In 1861 the United States Army numbered only seventeen thousand regular soldiers, most of whom were stationed in the west. Scott and John Wool, the Army's senior generals, were both in their seventies. The Confederacy, in order to defend its right to exist, had to build an army from scratch. Both sides called for volunteers, and within a matter of days a wave of patriotism swept tens of thousands of new recruits into uniform. In the four years of warfare that followed, some three million men took up arms.

The younger generals who emerged to lead the two armies knew one another's strengths and faults. Most had graduated from the Military Academy at West Point in New York, and many had fought in the Mexican War of 1846–1848. When the Civil War broke out, loyalties based on family ties often put former comrades-in-arms on opposing sides. Some military leaders rose to the occasion; others faltered. In the brief biographies that follow, you'll meet ten notable Southern generals. If you need help in putting Civil War events into their proper order, consult the map and time line on the following pages.

Northern vs. Southern States: a Comparison

CATEGORY	NORTHERN STATES (the Union)	SOUTHERN STATES (the Confederacy)
Population	Over 23,000,000; 4,070,000 men, ages 15–40.	Less than 10,000,000; 1,140,000 men, ages 15–40.
Area	24 states (West Virginia gained statehood in 1863); 670,000 square miles.	11 states; 780,000 square miles.
Manufacturing	110,000 shops and factories.	18,000 shops and factories.
Railroads	22,000 miles of track.	9,000 miles of track.
Major Crops	Corn, wheat, oats.	Cotton, tobacco, rice.
Financial Resources	80% of U.S. bank deposits. Paid for war with paper money backed by gold and silver.	20% of U.S. bank deposits. By war's end, Confederate paper money was nearly worthless.
Soldiers	2,100,000 men served in Union armies during the war.	800,000 men served in Confederate armies during the war.
Warships	90 in 1861; over 700 by war's end. Navy enforced crippling blockade of Southern ports.	0 in 1861. Built or purchased a small fleet of blockade runners and commerce raiders.

Maps of the Civil War

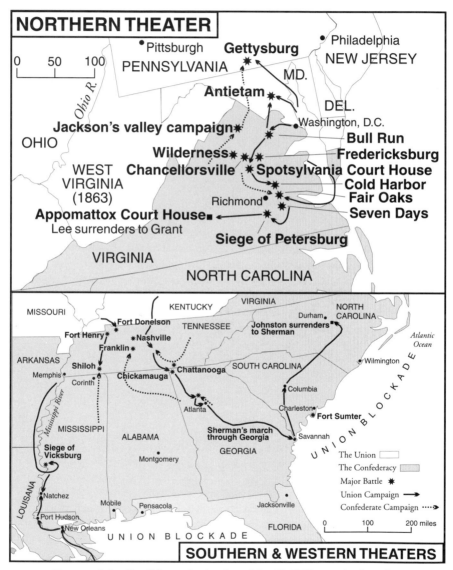

Dates and details of the major battles of the Civil War can be found in the "Time Line: Major Events of the Civil War" on the following pages.

TIME LINE:
Major Events of the Civil War

1820—*Missouri Compromise* balances the number of free and slave states; divides the west into free and slave territories at 36°30′.

1850—*Compromise of 1850* admits California as a free state; allows Utah and New Mexico to exercise popular sovereignty.

1854—*Kansas-Nebraska Bill* allows slavery north of 36°30′.

1856-1859—*Bleeding Kansas*: Proslavery and antislavery forces fight for the right to control Kansas.

1856—Rise of the antislavery Republican Party.

1857—Supreme Court's *Dred Scott* decision strikes down Missouri Compromise; declares that Congress cannot limit spread of slavery.

1859—*John Brown* raids federal arsenal at Harpers Ferry, Virginia. His plan to start a slave revolt fails.

1860—Lincoln elected president. South Carolina secedes from the Union.

1861—Southern states form Confederate States of America (CSA). Confederate troops fire on Fort Sumter in South Carolina (April 12–14).

First Battle of Bull Run (Virginia): Confederates drive back advancing Union forces (July 21).

1862—Union takes forts Henry and Donelson on Tennessee River (February 6–16).

Battle of Shiloh (Tennessee): Confederates win first day, but Union counterattack carries the decisive second day (April 6–7). Union naval forces capture New Orleans (April 25).

Jackson's Valley Campaign (Virginia): General Thomas "Stonewall" Jackson leads Confederate troops to a series of victories in the Shenandoah Valley (May 4–June 9).

Fair Oaks (Virginia): Union forces drive back the Confederates (May 31–June 1).

Seven Days (Virginia): Union forces threaten Richmond before being driven back by General Robert E. Lee (June 25–July 1).

Second Battle of Bull Run (Virginia): Another Southern victory helps the Confederacy regain most of Virginia (August 27–30).

Battle of Antietam (Maryland): Union army holds Lee's forces to a draw in bloodiest day of the war (September 17).

Battle of Fredericksburg (Virginia): Lee soundly defeats Union army led by General Ambrose Burnside (December 13).

1863—Lincoln's *Emancipation Proclamation* frees Southern slaves (Jan. 1).

Battle of Chancellorsville (Virginia): Southern victory marred by death of Stonewall Jackson (May 1–4).

Battle of Gettysburg (Pennsylvania): Greatest battle of the Civil War ends in defeat for Lee and his Southern troops (July 1–3).

Battle of Vicksburg (Mississippi): Confederate garrison surrenders after six-week siege, leaving entire Mississippi in Union hands (May 19–July 4).

Chickamauga (Georgia): Southern victory keeps Northern forces contained in Chattanooga (September 19–20).

Chattanooga campaign (Tennessee): Union victories at Lookout Mountain and Missionary Ridge open way into Georgia (November 23–25).

1864—*Battle of the Wilderness* (Virginia): Lee's victory does not stop General U. S. Grant from advancing on Petersburg and Richmond (May 5–6).

Spotsylvania Court House (Virginia): Another victory for Grant and his Northern forces (May 8–19).

Cold Harbor (Virginia): Lee's Southerners repulse Grant's assault, but the Northerners soon return to the offensive (June 1–3).

Siege of Petersburg (Virginia): Grant and Lee's forces battle for months; the North gradually wears down the outnumbered defenders (June 20, 1864–April 2, 1865).

Battle of Atlanta (Georgia): General William Sherman lays siege to Atlanta (July 17); the city falls on December 21.

March to the Sea: Sherman's troops cut a 40-mile wide swath as they advance to the Atlantic coast (November 16, 1864–February 18, 1865).

Franklin (Tennessee): Confederate troops led by General John Bell Hood are defeated and fail to cut Sherman's supply lines (November 30).

Nashville (Tennessee): Northern victory virtually ends the war in the west (December 15–16).

1865—Richmond falls to Grant's advancing army (April 3).

Appomattox Court House (Virginia): Lee surrenders to Grant (April 9).

Lincoln is shot by John Wilkes Booth (April 14).

North Carolina: Sherman accepts General Joe Johnston's surrender of the last major Southern army (April 26).

General Nathan Bedford Forrest

Nathan Bedford Forrest
(1821–1877)

The date was April 8, 1862. A Southern army was retreating from the bloody battleground at Shiloh, Tennessee. Colonel Nathan Bedford Forrest and his Mounted Rangers served as a rear guard. On a patch of ground called Fallen Timbers, they met an advancing Union force. True to his nature, Forrest ordered his outnumbered troopers to charge.

The Rangers galloped forward, yelling and firing shotguns. The Union troops turned and ran. A cavalry unit joined the panic, the riders trampling foot soldiers in their haste to escape. Sensing victory, Forrest raced ahead of his men. Behind him, the Confederates pulled up as fresh Union troops joined the battle.

All at once, Forrest found himself trapped in a sea of blue uniforms. Soldiers surged forward, hoping for a clear shot. Armed only with a sword and a pistol, Forrest tried to fight his way out. A bullet caught him just above the hip, leaving his leg numb. Still he raged on, turning his horse and breaking into the clear. In the same instant he reached down and jerked a Union soldier onto his horse. The man's comrades held their fire, giving Forrest time to spur his horse toward safety. He dumped his human shield as soon as he was out of rifle range.

Early Life

The daring horseman Nathan Bedford Forrest was born July 13, 1821, at Chapel Hill, Tennessee. He was a fraternal twin, the oldest son in a brood of eleven children. His blacksmith father moved the family to northern Mississippi thirteen years later. Like most frontier boys, Bedford spent more time doing farmwork than going to school. In all, his schooling added up to about six months. He later joked, "I never see a pen but what I think of a snake."[1]

After his father died in 1837, young Bedford took on a new role as head of the family. Those were hard times. Disease killed five of the children, including his twin sister. Bedford spent long days plowing, planting, and weeding. At night he sat up late, making buckskin leggings, shoes, and caps for his siblings. Somehow, he vowed, he would escape the drudgery of farm life.

Forrest was twenty-one when he went to work for an uncle who ran a stable in Hernando, Mississippi. Despite his lack of schooling, Forrest proved to have a good head for business. As for courage, he proved his coolness under fire the day four men gunned down his uncle. He shot two of the men and drove off the others with a knife. From that day on, he was a local hero.

In 1845 Forrest married Mary Ann Montgomery. Six years later the couple moved to Memphis, where Forrest traded in cotton, real estate, and slaves. He also served a year as a Memphis alderman. Profits from the slave trade allowed him to buy two plantations. The purchase fulfilled his dream of joining the wealthy planter class. In 1859 Forrest moved his wife and two children to Green Grove plantation in Coahama County, Mississippi. By then his estate was worth over a million dollars.

The Civil War

Forrest was almost forty when the Civil War started in 1861. He was a tall, hot-tempered man who stood a muscular six feet two inches tall. His blue-gray eyes glittered and his iron-gray hair and black beard were well kept. No one could have guessed that he possessed a gift for leading men in battle.

When Tennessee left the Union, Forrest joined the Mounted Rangers as a private. Along with his brother and his son Willie, he trained at Camp Yellowjack. His leadership skills surfaced as he drilled beside younger men. The governor promoted Forrest to lieutenant colonel and asked him to raise a regiment of cavalry. Forrest recruited 500 men—but most lacked rifles and horses. He solved the problem by spending his own money to equip his troopers. Next came the drills. Unlike most cavalry leaders, Forrest trained his men to fight on foot, as well as from horseback.

By mid-November, the unit was ready to fight. Forrest led an attack on a Union wagon train and seized a supply of much-needed blankets. Late in December he engaged a larger Union force in Kentucky. When the Bluecoats tried to stand and fight, Forrest made a lightning decision. Dividing his men, he routed the Bluecoats by hitting them from the center and on both flanks. His men began to call him the "Wizard of the Saddle."

In February 1862 Forrest and his men were based at Fort Donelson in Tennessee. When a Union force laid siege to the fort, the Southern commander felt compelled to surrender. Forrest was made of sterner stuff. He saddled up before dawn and led 1,300 men to safety by fording a deep, icy creek. Inspired by these exploits, the Third Tennessee Cavalry made him its colonel. A few days later the regiment fought in the rear guard at the Battle of Shiloh.

The painful wound he received at Shiloh healed quickly, and Forrest returned to duty. Reports of his exploits brought a promotion to brigadier general. On July 13 his new brigade pinned down a Union force at Murfreesboro. Forrest called for a brief truce, which he used to demand a speedy surrender. Fight on, he warned, and he would put every Northerner to the sword. The threat was a bluff, but it sounded real enough. The Union commander surrendered his twelve hundred troops plus $500,000 in supplies and equipment.[2]

Forrest's success in training cavalry units led the Confederate government to ask him to try again. His ads promised, "Come on, boys, if you want a heap of fun and to kill some Yankees."[3] Recruits rushed to join him, and he put them to work almost at once. In December 1863 Forrest braved winter cold and muddy roads to lead a raid into western Tennessee. When they weren't ambushing Bluecoats, his troopers burned bridges and tore up railroad tracks.

Forrest fought his battles in a red-hot blaze of emotion. After General Braxton Bragg failed to exploit his victory at Chickamauga, Forrest was enraged. Legend says that he told Bragg, "You have played the part of a scoundrel, and if you were any part of a man, I would slap your jaws. . . . If you ever again try to interfere with me or cross my path, it will be at peril of your life."[4] The high command solved the conflict by giving Forrest an independent command.

In April 1864 Forrest led an attack on Fort Pillow, Tennessee. Fighting in the front lines, he had three horses shot from under him. As his troops

Nathan Bedford Forrest was a master of hit-and-run cavalry tactics. His troopers routed larger Northern units by attacking and fighting with reckless zeal. To further disrupt enemy plans, Forrest's men cut telegraph lines, tore up railroad tracks, and burned supply trains.

tightened their iron ring around the fort, he called on the fort to surrender. This time the Union commander refused, and Forrest ordered an assault. His men burst over the stockade walls, sending the defenders fleeing in panic. A hundred or more Union soldiers, some white and many black, were shot as they tried to surrender. Northerners later charged that Forrest had ordered the massacre. Whether or not he did, the slaughter did not disturb him. "The river was dyed with the blood . . . for 200 yards," he reported. "It is hoped that these facts will demonstrate . . . that negro soldiers cannot cope with Southerners."[5]

Early in June, Forrest caught a Union force strung out on a muddy Mississippi road. His 3,500 men routed 8,000 Union troops and captured 200 wagons. The Union general later claimed he had been hit by at least 15,000 Confederates. Forrest next destroyed a huge Union supply base at Johnsonville, Tennessee. The Federals shook off the losses and drove General John Hood out of Atlanta in December.

Hood enlisted Forrest to spearhead an ill-fated drive into central Tennessee. Forrest fought with his usual dash, but the Confederates were beaten at Franklin and Nashville. After Nashville, his cavalry shielded Hood's troops as they withdrew into Mississippi. In February, Forrest was given the rank of lieutenant general. He was still leading raids on Union outposts when the war ended two months later.

Forrest's Legacy

Forrest lived a charmed life all through the Civil War. During combat he killed or wounded at least thirty Union soldiers. His foes shot twenty-nine horses out from under him. He survived four wounds and countless hardships. When it was over, he turned his talents to peacetime pursuits.

Times were hard in the postwar South. Forrest said, "I went into the army worth a million and a half dollars and came out a beggar."[6] In 1868 he poured money and energy into building the Selma, Marion, and Memphis Railroad. The debt-ridden line never made a profit.

In 1867 the Ku Klux Klan chose Forrest as its Grand Wizard. He believed that Southern whites and their way of life should be protected from the forces of Reconstruction. When the secret society turned violent, Forrest ordered its members to disband. The Klan survived, but without its colorful leader.

Sickness at last claimed the life that Union bullets could not. Forrest fell ill with diabetes and died in his sleep on October 29, 1877. Thousands of his comrades-in-arms marched in the funeral procession. Today soldiers still quote Nathan Bedford Forrest's rule for winning battles. Asked how he explained his success at Murfreesboro, Forrest said, "I just took the short cut and got there first with the most men."[7]

William Joseph Hardee
(1815–1873)

In March 1865 the Civil War was almost over. In Virginia the Union army was inching toward Richmond. In the Deep South, General William Sherman's troops had looted and burned their way to the sea. After pausing at Savannah, Sherman headed north. General Joe Johnston, outnumbered three to one, called on General William Hardee to stop the Northerners.

Hardee's corps had been whittled down by desertions and illness. Many men had never seen combat. Yet near Bentonville, North Carolina, on March 19, "Old Reliable" led 13,700 men in a bold attack on Sherman's left wing. Johnston, an old friend, wrote, "Hardee, after commanding the double-quick, led the charge. . . . With his knightly gallantry [he]

General William Joseph Hardee

dashed over the enemy breastworks on horseback, in front of his men."[1]

The Union soldiers drew back as the inspired Southern soldiers battered their defenses. Seeing his men strung out across the battlefield, Hardee ordered a pause to regroup. His caution gave the Union forces time to mount a counterattack. The Southerners held their ground, but could advance no farther.

Sunset brought an end to the day's fighting. That was when Hardee learned the full cost of his victory. His only son, sixteen-year-old Willie, had been killed by a Union bullet early in the day.

Early Life

William Joseph Hardee was born near Savannah, Georgia, on October 12, 1815. The youngest of seven children, William grew up on his father's plantation. Because there were no schools close by, the Hardees hired a tutor to teach their children. When it came time to plan his future, the boy chose an army career. He qualified for the United States Military Academy, but had to wait four years for an opening. When he was admitted in 1834, Hardee was eager to begin. At graduation in 1838 he ranked in the middle of his class.

The army sent Hardee to fight with the Second Dragoons in the Seminole War. He saw little action, and in 1839 he fell ill. During his treatment at a hospital in St. Augustine, he met and married

Elizabeth Dummett. The army next dispatched the young officer to France for a year to study military tactics. During the Mexican War (1846–1848) Captain Hardee took part in the invasion of northern Mexico. The Mexicans captured him, but released him as part of a prisoner exchange. Free once more, Hardee fought under General Zachary Taylor at Veracruz, Contreras, and Molino del Rey. His courage under fire earned two battlefield promotions.

After the war Hardee commanded a force of dragoons and Texas Rangers on the Texas frontier. After chasing Comanches for a time, he was recalled to Washington. There he wrote a textbook called *Rifle and Light Infantry Tactics.* After it went into print, the book became must reading throughout the army. He also designed an improved hat for cavalry troopers.

Tragedy struck in 1853 when his wife died, leaving Hardee with four motherless children. An aunt took in the children while Hardee pursued his army career. In 1856 the War Department named Lieutenant Colonel Hardee as commandant of cadets at West Point. He was still serving at the military academy when the war started in 1861.

The Civil War

When Georgia left the Union, Hardee resigned from the army and offered his services to the Confederacy. The new government gave him the rank of colonel and sent him to Mobile, Alabama. Hardee could see that the port city's defenses at Fort Morgan had to be strengthened. He handled the project with quiet competence.

When Confederate troops beat the Union army at the First Battle of Bull Run, the South rejoiced. Numbers did not count, Southerners bragged, because "one Confederate can whip half-a-dozen Yanks." Hardee knew better. His training and experience told him that the South faced a long, grim struggle. Soldiers needed shoes, uniforms, food, guns, and bullets. All were in short supply in the South.

Hardee also knew that soldiers fought best when they had faith in their officers. When he took command of a unit, he picked the best staff officers he could find. Like all good leaders, he worked to build confidence and respect in his soldiers. "Old Reliable" soon won acclaim for leading well-drilled troops to the right place at the right time.[2]

The South needed trained officers, and promotions came quickly. In June 1861, newly promoted to brigadier general, Hardee went to Arkansas. There he arranged the transfer of the state's regiments to Confederate command. During the summer he led those units in a series of skirmishes along the Missouri border. A visitor described him as "a handsome man of a very striking figure . . . courteous and pleasant in manner."[3] That fall, newly promoted to major general, he joined General Albert Sidney Johnston in Kentucky as a corps commander.

Major General U. S. Grant's Union troops advanced south from Tennessee in the spring of 1862. Johnston organized a surprise attack that struck the Federals near Shiloh, Tennessee, on April 6. Hardee's corps swept forward and broke through the right side of the Union lines. With a major victory within their grasp, the Southerners paused to rest and regroup. Some of the men slipped away to loot captured Union stores.

During the night 20,000 fresh Union troops showed up. Grant threw his reinforcements into a fierce counterattack. As Hardee rallied his men, he and his horse were hit. Shrugging, he dismissed his arm wound as a "slight scratch."[4] In four years of fighting, it was the only wound he received. Many of his men were less fortunate. One brigade started the battle with 2,750 men. By the end of the second day, only 58 were fit for duty.

The beaten Southerners limped south into Alabama. In July, Hardee led his men north to join General Braxton Bragg's Army of Tennessee. Promoted to lieutenant general, corps commander Hardee won his most notable victory that December. On the final day of 1862, his corps found a weakness on the right flank of the Union lines near Murfreesboro, Tennessee. The Southerners broke through and advanced three miles before stopping to set up a defense line. Bragg, fearing a counterattack, failed to follow up the breakthrough. Two days later the battle ended in a stalemate. The Confederates lost ten thousand men; the Federals suffered thirteen thousand casualties.

Hardee joined a group of officers who challenged Bragg's fitness to lead. The squabbling poisoned relations between the two men. Worse, it hampered the campaign and lowered troop morale. Any chance of saving the South's position in the west vanished as the year sped by. Hardee used his free time to woo and marry plantation owner Mary Foreman Lewis.

In November the Confederates stumbled into a golden chance to destroy a Union army at Chattanooga. Once again Bragg was slow to act. The delay gave the Union troops time to mount a new attack. Hardee commanded the army's right flank, but this time the Bluecoats hit the left flank at Missionary Ridge. When the Southern lines broke, Hardee had no choice but to retreat. He saved his corps by staging a rare night withdrawal.

Bragg resigned after the defeat. As senior officer, Hardee took command of the Army of Tennessee. He did not want the post, but he threw himself into the task of rebuilding the shattered army. When General Joe Johnston arrived to take his place, Hardee gladly returned to his corps.

In 1864 Hardee's corps fought in the battles that ended with the fall of Atlanta. He then tried to defend Savannah, but Sherman's large, well-supplied army drove him out of the city in December.

Three Confederate soldiers, captured in battle, wait for Union officers to decide their future. If they were lucky, they were paroled and allowed to return home. Less-fortunate prisoners were sent to overcrowded prison camps, where thousands died of hunger and disease.

Hardee's skillful retreat into the Carolinas only delayed the South's final defeat. In March 1865 he led his troops in their last-gasp charge at Bentonville.

Hardee's Legacy

A month later the war was over. After leading the Army of Tennessee south to be disbanded, Hardee rode to his wife's plantation near Demopolis, Alabama. Mary and his daughters were waiting for him in a log cabin. The soldier-turned-farmer arranged a sharecropping system for the seventy-five former slaves who worked the land. Together, Hardee and his workers raised cotton, corn, mules, and hogs.

In 1866 the family moved to Selma, Alabama. Hardee became active in warehousing and insurance. He also served as president of the Selma and Meridian Railroad. The railroad lost money, and Hardee lost control in 1869. In good times and bad, he was always well groomed. He never left his room without his coat—except when he was gardening.

To escape the heat, the Hardees spent their summers at White Sulphur Springs, West Virginia. Hardee fell ill there in 1873, and doctors advised against the long train trip home. The stalwart corps commander died in Wythesville, Virginia, on November 6. True to his wishes, Mary took him home for burial in Selma's Live Oak Cemetery. Veterans and friends gathered to pay their respects in "the greatest public demonstration known at a funeral in Alabama."[5]

General Ambrose Powell Hill

Ambrose Powell Hill
(1825–1865)

General Robert E. Lee led the Army of Virginia northward in September 1862. After Lee's battle plans fell into Union hands, General George McClellan acted quickly. His army, eighty-seven thousand strong moved toward Sharpsburg, Maryland. Lee was waiting at Antietam Creek with thirty-five thousand soldiers. To reinforce his lines, he sent for General A. P. Hill.

Hill was seventeen miles away, mopping up after winning a major victory at Harpers Ferry. Lee's orders arrived at 6:30 A.M. on September 17. Within the hour, Hill had five brigades of his Light Division on the road to Antietam. Hundreds of exhausted men dropped out during the forced march, but Hill drove the others onward. They heard the rumble of gunfire as they neared Antietam Creek.

Union troops were surging forward, ready to crush Lee's thinly-held right wing. At the last moment, Hill's three thousand troops rushed in, screeching a fierce Confederate yell. Hill, clad in his trademark red shirt, waved his sword and urged his men forward. The withering Confederate fire forced the Bluecoats to pull back. McClellan refused to risk a second assault, leaving Lee free to withdraw in good order. Hill's heroic seven-hour march had saved the Confederates from a crushing defeat.

Early Life

Ambrose Powell Hill was born near Petersburg, Virginia, on November 9, 1825. Powell, as his mother called him, was the much-loved youngest child of an old Virginia family. The baby grew up to be self-reliant, bright, and forceful. Despite his slight build, he was a fine horseman. After attending the neighborhood school, he went on to the Black Hill Seminary. Inspired by family tales of military heroism, he decided to become a soldier. Powell was sixteen when he entered the United States Military Academy in 1842.

The first of the many illnesses that troubled Hill's adult life struck during his third year at West Point. He recovered during a long stay at home but was forced to repeat the year. When war broke out in 1846, Hill had to stand by as his former classmates left for Mexico. He graduated in June 1847, just in time to join General Winfield Scott's army as it entered Mexico City. After the war, Lieutenant Hill served with the First Artillery Regiment as a supply officer.

Hill served in Florida during the Seminole Wars until he fell ill with yellow fever. In the fall of 1855 the army assigned him to work with the United States Coast Survey. Twice he became engaged, and twice his fiancées broke the engagements. One of the young women married his good friend and West Point roommate George McClellan. Finally, in 1859, Hill took Dolly Morgan McClung to the altar. Dolly gave him four daughters, but only two survived childhood.

From his post in Washington, D.C., Hill could see the Civil War approaching. He disliked slavery, but he would not turn his back on Virginia. On March 1, 1861, he resigned from the army and offered his sword to the South.

The Civil War

The Confederacy did not give Powell Hill the general's rank he craved. Instead, he was sworn in as a colonel and assigned to the 13th Virginia Volunteer Regiment. The unit's quick improvement in organization and discipline proved Hill's talents. He could be stern, but his men loved him for his courage and his devotion to their well-being. Superior officers sometimes found him hard to handle. While on the road that led to Antietam, Hill had a run-in with the quick-tempered Stonewall Jackson. When Hill

A. P. Hill and his Light Division were only one of the Southern units that fought heroically at Antietam. Some of the Civil War's fiercest fighting took place at this stone bridge over Antietam Creek. Four hundred men of the Light Division upset the Union plans by holding off a force of 12,500 Bluecoats for nearly three hours before the Confederates fell back.

would not back down, Jackson put him under arrest. Happily for the South, he relented in time for Hill to play a major role in the campaign.

The longhaired, bearded Hill was easy to spot among the gray-clad Southerners. Instead of a standard jacket, he dressed for battle in a bright red shirt. He also rode equipped with a revolver, sword, field glasses, and a pipe. Soldiers called him "Little Powell," most likely because he carried only 145 pounds on his five foot ten inch frame. His hazel eyes were keen and bright.

General Joe Johnston noted Hill's leadership skills and added the Third Tennessee Regiment to the Virginian's command. In July 1861 a Southern army under General Pierre Beauregard met an invading Union army near Manassas, Virginia. Hill and his men were held in reserve on the Confederate right flank. They cheered as Confederate troops routed the Bluecoats in the First Battle of Bull Run.

In February 1862 Hill received his brigadier general's stars. That spring the Union army was advancing toward Richmond from the southeast. In May at Williamsburg, Hill gave his new brigade its first taste of war. His well-drilled soldiers turned back a Union thrust, capturing 160 prisoners and seven battle flags. A battle report paid tribute to Hill's unit: "Its organization was perfect throughout the battle, and it was marched off the field in as good order as it entered it."[1]

Later that month, Hill was promoted to major general and took command of the Light Division. He whipped his soldiers into a fast-marching, hard-hitting unit. The division was guarding bridges north of Richmond when General Robert E. Lee took command of the Army of Virginia. True to his nature, Lee took the offensive. He ordered an attack for the morning of June 26.

When 3:00 P.M. came and no one else had moved, Hill ordered his men forward. The Light Division suffered heavy losses, but drove the Union line back to the village of Mechanicsville. That firefight led to a series of battles known as the Seven Days. When the smoke cleared, the Southerners had driven the Union forces from the area. Hill, Lee wrote, "met this large [Federal] force with the impetuous courage for which that officer and his troops are distinguished."[2]

From that day on Hill took part in every major eastern battle. In 1862 his troops helped win major victories at Cedar Mountain and the Second Battle of Bull Run. He could not repeat his Antietam success at Fredericksburg, where his troops suffered heavy casualties three months later. In May 1863, after Jackson was mortally wounded at Chancellorsville, Hill took command of the Second Corps. Moments later Lee lost another corps commander. Hill went down with wounds in both calves.

Lee led his army into Pennsylvania in June 1863. Back in the saddle and promoted to lieutenant general, Hill now commanded the new Third Corps. Told that there was a warehouse full of shoes in Gettysburg, he sent seven thousand men to collect them. On July 1, Hill's soldiers ran into some Union troops and drove them from the town. Hill, who was ill and out of touch with events, did not pursue the beaten enemy. Critics later found fault with him for starting a battle and then failing to follow up his advantage. By the time the main battle began, the Union troops could not be dislodged. Lee was forced to retreat southward.

By the summer of 1864 the tide of war had turned. General U. S. Grant pinned the Army of Virginia into its trenches near Richmond. In February 1865, kidney problems confined Hill to his bed. He returned from sick leave in March, a short time before Grant broke through the Southern lines near Petersburg. As the battle raged, Hill conferred briefly with Lee, then rode out to inspect the lines. He and his aide were chasing a band of Union stragglers when the Bluecoats opened fire. A .58-caliber bullet hit Hill in the chest. He was dead before he hit the ground.

Hill's Legacy

The entire Southern line was under attack when news of Hill's death reached Lee. It was a bitter loss, for Little Powell ranked high on the South's roster of generals. "He is at rest now," Lee said, "and we who are left are the ones to suffer."[3] Years later, as he lay dying, Lee's thoughts may have turned once more to Hill. In his delirium the grand old man is said to have cried out, "Tell Hill he must come up!" Stonewall Jackson died with a similar order on his lips. Soon after he was wounded at Chancellorsville, Jackson called out, "Order A. P. Hill to prepare for action."[4]

Jefferson Davis, president of the Confederacy, learned of Hill's death just before he fled from Richmond. "He was," Davis said, "brave and skillful, and always ready to . . . do his full duty. A truer, more devoted, self-sacrificing soldier never lived or died."[5]

Virginia did not forget its favorite son. In 1892, with its economy on the mend, the state chose Richmond as the site of a statue dedicated to the memory of A. P. Hill. It was only the fourth Civil War monument the South had placed in its wartime capital.

John Bell Hood
(1821–1879)

In May 1864 General William Sherman's Union troops were inching toward Atlanta. Confederate General Joe Johnston used delaying tactics to keep Sherman off balance. Up north in Richmond, Confederate President Jefferson Davis lost patience. In that dark hour he replaced Johnston with General John Bell Hood.

Despite a mangled arm and the loss of a leg, the giant Texan was full of fight. After Sherman forced him out of Atlanta, Hood led the remnants of the Army of Tennessee northward. On November 30, he attacked a Union force at Franklin, south of Nashville. Time after time the gallant Southerners charged the Union lines. Time after time they were thrown back.

General John Bell Hood

Hood regrouped and moved on to lay siege to Nashville. This time it was the Union troops who attacked. On December 15 General George Thomas's men bent Hood's left flank. That night Hood pulled back to a stronger line along the Overton Hills. Thomas renewed the attack the next day.

The Southern troops repulsed every Union charge. By four o'clock Hood began to think he had won the day. His hopes died when a hard-pressed Florida brigade gave way. As Union troops surged forward, Hood's entire center broke and ran.

Thomas's men chased what remained of the Confederate army southward. When the pressure ended at last, Hood asked to be relieved of his command. Jefferson Davis granted his request.

Early Life

John Bell Hood was born at Owingsville, Kentucky, on June 29, 1821. His prominent family believed strongly in the Southern way of life. As a boy, Hood was more interested in riding, hunting, and fishing than he was in classwork. He grew up to be a giant of a man, fearless and headstrong. Women liked his blond good looks, his blue eyes, and his booming, musical voice.

John's father wanted him to study medicine, but the boy yearned for an army career. His uncle, Congressman Richard French, secured him an appointment to the United States Military Academy.

Hood entered West Point in 1849 and graduated in 1853. Bookwork was not his strong point—he graduated near the bottom of his class.

After a brief tour of duty in California, Lieutenant Hood transferred to the Second Cavalry in Missouri. Orders soon sent the regiment riding across Arkansas to Fort Mason, Texas. For the next four years, Hood and his fellow soldiers stood guard along the frontier. Hood greatly admired the regiment's best soldier, Lieutenant Colonel Robert E. Lee. In 1857 he earned praise for his conduct during a fight with Comanches. When an arrow pierced his hand, he calmly broke off the arrowhead and pulled the shaft free.

As war drew near, Hood cast his lot with Texas and the South. He resigned from the United States Army on April 16, 1861, and traveled to Richmond, Virginia. There he offered his services to the Confederacy. The belles of the city took him into their hearts. The army made him a captain of cavalry. Promotions came quickly—and so did the criticism.

The Civil War

History has not been kind to John Bell Hood. No one doubts his courage or his genius for inspiring the men he led. When his Texans went into battle, their war cry was "Hood! Hood! Hood!"[1] His critics, however, charge him with being rash and erratic. He was a superb corps commander they say, who should never have gone higher. Whatever his faults, Hood paid a high price for his gallantry. At Gettysburg, Union gunfire cost him the use of his left arm and hand. In the battle of Chickamauga, he lost his right leg. For the rest of the war, his men strapped him to his horse each day so that he could ride.

By March 1862, Hood had been promoted to brigadier general. On June 27, as commander of the Texas Brigade, he fought beside General Lee. During the battle of Gaines's Mill, Lee asked Hood if he could break a strong Union position. The Texan replied, "I will try."[2] An inspired assault by the Texas Brigade carried the day.

Hood's headstrong ways sometimes landed him in hot water. During the early days of Lee's 1862 thrust into Maryland, Hood's troops captured some Union ambulances. Ordered to turn them over to the army's quartermaster, Hood refused. After General James Longstreet heard the news, he ordered Hood's arrest. When Lee next saw the Texas Brigade, the men were chanting, "We want Hood! Give us Hood!"[3] Lee, fearing that the brigade would refuse to fight, suspended the arrest. Hood buckled on his sword and led his cheering soldiers into a series of bloody assaults.

In October, at Stonewall Jackson's urging, Hood was promoted to major general. His new rank gave him command of a division in Longstreet's corps. When the Confederates met invading Union troops at Fredericksburg, Virginia, Hood and his men were dug in on the hills behind the town. Now it was the

A Southern officer drawn to resemble John Bell Hood (right foreground) urges his men to hold firm against a Union assault. Some of his soldiers are ready to throw crude hand grenades at the oncoming Union soldiers. Hood, who later lost a leg at Chickamagua, once warned Northern invaders, "We will fight you to the death."

Federals who charged into heavy fire. When the guns fell silent, twelve thousand Bluecoats lay dead or wounded on the battlefield. For once, Hood showed restraint. He held his men in check when every instinct urged him to pursue the retreating Northerners.

On July 2, 1863, Hood's troops played a key role in the Battle of Gettysburg. Across from his lines at the southern end of the battlefield lay Little Round Top. If Hood's troops captured the hill, they would be in position to rake the entire Union line. Hours passed as Lee waited for Longstreet to begin the attack. When Longstreet at last gave the order, it was almost five o'clock. Hood and his men ran headlong into a firestorm. A shell fragment shattered Hood's arm and knocked him off his horse. Given time to prepare, the Federals had built up their strength. As the next day proved, the delay cost the South its best chance of winning one of the war's key battles.

By September 1863 Hood was back in action, this time in Tennessee. Rushed into battle at Chickamauga Creek, he was wounded a second time. This bullet cost him a leg. His troops raised $5,000 to buy him a hand-crafted leg, but the war would not wait. A one-legged Hood was back in the saddle early in 1864. Now he wore the three stars of a lieutenant general.

In July, Confederate President Davis picked Hood to replace Johnston as commander of the Army of Tennessee. Davis pinned his hopes for saving Atlanta on Hood's aggressive style. True to his nature, Hood quickly carried the battle to General Sherman's oncoming Union forces. On July 20 and 24, he launched attacks that were repulsed with heavy losses. After Sherman cut his supply line in late August, Hood knew Atlanta was lost. He burned his supplies and abandoned the city.

Hood led his army northward, recruiting soldiers and laying plans for a new campaign. By this time many of his forty thousand men were marching bare-foot. Food and ammunition were running low. Despite the odds against him, Hood pushed on. He laid plans to cut Sherman's supply line northwest of Chattanooga. The crushing defeats at Franklin and Nashville in December ended his hopes and his army career. Hood's bedraggled soldiers knew only that they wanted "Uncle Joe" Johnston back. On the way south they sang this sad little song:

> *And now I'm going southward,*
> *My heart is full of woe.*
> *I'm going back to Georgia*
> *To see my Uncle Joe.*[4]

Hood's Legacy

Freed of his duties, Hood spent the summer of 1865 in Texas. Friends began a campaign to buy him a home in San Antonio. Hood settled in New Orleans instead. To start a business, he borrowed $250 from each of forty friends. The bankroll allowed him to buy and sell cotton and other goods on commission. As his business prospered, Hood also bought a life insurance company.

After a lifetime of brief romances, Hood settled down at last. He married Anna Marie Hennan, daughter of a leading Louisiana family. The marriage produced a small population boom. Over the next eleven years Anna gave birth to eleven children, including three sets of twins.

To restore his image, Hood wrote a memoir that was published as *Advance and Retreat.* The book strongly defended his actions at Atlanta and Nashville. He was only forty-eight when yellow fever struck his family in 1879. After watching Anna and his oldest daughter die, General Hood fell ill on August 27. Three days later he was dead.

In 1864 Robert E. Lee had noted his friend's strengths and failings. In a letter to Jefferson Davis, Lee wrote, "Hood is a good fighter, very industrious on the battlefield, careless off, and I have had no opportunity of judging his action when the whole responsibility rested upon him. I have a high opinion of his gallantry, earnestness and zeal."

General Thomas "Stonewall" Jackson

Thomas "Stonewall" Jackson
(1824–1863)

The first major battle of the Civil War took place in Virginia near a stream known as Bull Run. The Union forces opened the long bloody day by hitting hard at the Confederate left wing. General Pierre Beauregard shifted troops to meet the attack. General Thomas Jackson's brigade took its place on Henry Hill.

Jackson's 6,500 gray-clad Virginians had been marching for two days and nights. Calmly, the newly promoted general positioned his weary troops. When the Bluecoats attacked, they threw 18,000 men at the Southern line.

The smoke and tumult of battle left Jackson unruffled. Mounted on his favorite horse, Little Sorrel, he urged his men to make every shot count.

As the firing grew in volume, he raised his left hand to signal. An instant later, shrapnel gashed his middle finger. Jackson wrapped a cloth around the finger and returned to his duties.

Brigadier General Barnard Bee's brigade was fighting for its life near Jackson's men. "Rally behind the Virginians," Bee cried. "There is Jackson standing like a stone wall."[1] The line held, and the Union advance faltered as fresh Southern troops appeared. The Bluecoats backed away and then fled.

As news of the victory spread, Southerners applauded their new hero. Tom Jackson, the modest college professor, had earned a new nickname. From that day on everyone called him "Stonewall" Jackson.

Early Life

The baby who became Stonewall Jackson was born at Clarksburg, Virginia, on January 21, 1824. By the time young Thomas Jonathan was seven, both his parents were dead. He and his sister, Laura, went to live with their uncle, Cummins Jackson. When Tom was nine, he and his brother, Warren, floated down the Ohio River on a raft. They paid for their adventure by selling firewood to river steamers.

As a teenager, Tom placed second in an exam for the United States Military Academy. When the winner dropped out, Tom took his place. The shy eighteen-year-old soon found that hard work could not hide the gaps in his schooling. He almost flunked out. Then, slowly, his efforts began to pay off. At graduation in 1846 he ranked seventeenth in his class.

The United States went to war with Mexico that same year. At Churubusco, Lieutenant Jackson took command of his unit when his captain was killed. During the attack on Chapultepec, Jackson loaded and fired a cannon after all the gunners were killed. His performance earned a promotion to major.

After serving in the Seminole War, Jackson took a teaching job at the Virginia Military Institute (VMI) in 1851. The cadets chafed under his strict rules and thought his lectures were boring. They laughed at his religious fervor and called him "Tom Fool" behind his back. During his years at VMI, Jackson married twice. His first wife died fourteen months into their marriage. He remarried in 1857, only to face a second tragedy. The couple's first child died soon after she was born.

When the war started, Jackson marched the cadets to Richmond to enlist. Sworn in with the rank of colonel, he was sent to Harpers Ferry. In a short time he turned a horde of raw recruits into well-drilled troops. Discipline, he knew, would pay off in the battles to come.

The Civil War

A slender five feet ten inches tall, Jackson did not look like a hero. He sat his saddle carelessly, and during a battle he often sucked on a lemon. He did not like to fight on Sundays, and he neither drank nor cursed.

On a July day in 1862 he came face-to-face with his reputation. Slowed down by a road clogged with wagons, Jackson took a shortcut through a field of oats. Moments later an angry farmer stopped him. The farmer's scowl gave way to a smile when he learned Jackson's name. "Hurrah for Stonewall Jackson!" he shouted. "By God, General, please do me the honor to ride all over my damned old oats!"[2]

After the First Battle of Bull Run, Jackson's sudden fame brought him a promotion and a new task. In October, Major General Jackson rode west to harry a Union force that was sweeping through the Shenandoah Valley. After Jackson hit Kernstown in March 1862, the Union sent three corps to stop him. Jackson, with only 17,000 men, used speed and surprise to balance the odds. In the time frame of forty days his "foot cavalry" covered 400 miles and fought five battles. The raids tied up 40,000 Union soldiers, men Union General George McClellan thought he needed for his advance on Richmond.

In late June, Jackson slipped out of the valley and marched east. Lee needed his help because McClellan was threatening Richmond. When McClellan delayed his attack, Lee sent Jackson to launch a counterattack. For once, nothing seemed to go right. Worn down in body and spirit, Jackson's troops arrived at Mechanicsville a day late. A missed turn cost him two hours on the road to Gaines's Mill. At Malvern Hill, a deadly Union artillery barrage cut down two thousand of his men.

The devastation left behind by a Civil War battle shows clearly in this photo of dead horses and smashed artillery caissons (wheeled vehicles shown). Stonewall Jackson earned his nickname by calmly directing his "foot cavalry" through the deadly barrage of bullets and artillery shells that left scenes like this one behind.

Jackson was back in top form when he took the field against a Union force led by General John Pope. On August 9, the two armies fought to a draw at Cedar Mountain. When Lee learned that fresh Union troops were coming, he sent Jackson to cut Pope's supply line. Two days later Jackson's 20,000 men smashed the Union supply base at Manassas Junction. Pope wheeled in pursuit and caught Jackson near Bull Run Creek on August 29. Jackson held his ground, giving Lee time to join him. The Second Battle of Bull Run ended like the first, with the Southerners triumphant.

Lee believed the time was ripe to take the war into the North. As he headed into Maryland, Jackson split off to attack the twelve thousand Union troops at Harpers Ferry. A fierce artillery barrage demolished the Northern defenses. Within hours Jackson was marching through the night toward Antietam Creek. He found Lee dug in on a ridge above the creek. McClellan, it turned out, had moved quickly for once. On September 17, Jackson and his men stood their ground on Lee's left wing. When the smoke cleared, both sides were bloodied and weary. Lee called off the invasion.

Promoted to lieutenant general in October, Jackson took command of Lee's Second Corps. Two months later he led his corps at Fredericksburg, where 78,500 Confederates faced 122,000 Bluecoats. When Lee asked him if he could hold against so many, Jackson did not hesitate. "My men have sometimes failed to *take* a position," he said, "but to *defend* one, never."[3] On December 13 his corps beat back a morning attack by 50,000 Union troops.

In the spring of 1863 General Joseph Hooker moved westward, hoping to outflank Lee's army. Lee saw the move as a chance to try a daring plan. While General Jubal Early held the line at Fredericksburg with a small force, Jackson set off to strike Hooker's southern flank. Somehow he moved 28,000 soldiers through dense woods without being spotted. At 5:15 P.M. on May 2, Jackson ordered a charge. The Southerners surged forward, screaming the Confederate yell. Caught by surprise, the Bluecoats dropped their cooking pots and fled.

That night Jackson set out on a scouting trip. After riding close to the Union outposts, he turned back toward his own lines. Nervous North Carolina troops mistook his party for an enemy unit and opened fire. Three bullets struck Jackson and sent Little Sorrel plunging out of control. When his men reached him, blood was spurting from his left arm. They carried him to a field hospital, where surgeons removed the arm.

At first the iron-willed Jackson seemed certain to survive. A few days later, however, a head cold turned into pneumonia. Calm as always, Jackson prepared to die. On May 10, 1863, he spoke for the last time. "Let us cross over the river," he muttered, "and rest under the shade of the trees."[4]

Jackson's Legacy

Told of Jackson's wound, Lee knew at once the depth of his loss. "He has lost his left arm, but I have lost my right arm," he sighed.[5]

Two months later, at Gettysburg, the words took on a new meaning. On July 1, Lee urged Stonewall's replacement, General Richard Ewell, to attack the Union's exposed northern flank. Jackson would have moved at once. Ewell waited a day. The delay gave the Federals time to strengthen their lines, and Ewell's attack failed. The stage was set for Pickett's doomed charge and the Confederate loss at Gettysburg.

Military experts still study Stonewall Jackson's battles. The quiet Virginian was gifted with a supreme sense of how best to position his men for battle. In an age when few generals knew how to keep secrets, Jackson shared his plans with no one. Time after time, his brigades seemed to appear out of nowhere to hit Union troops with stunning force.

Jackson inspired love and trust in his own troops. The man they called "Old Jack" drove them hard, but they followed where he led. On a freezing winter night in 1862, a soldier crowded close to a campfire. "I wish the Yankees were in Hell!" he cried.

A friend shook his head. "I don't," he growled. "Old Jack would follow them there, with our brigade in front!"[6]

Joe Johnston
(1807–1891)

The South honored only a handful of men with the rank of full (four-star) general during the Civil War. Everyone knows the name Robert E. Lee, but few remember Joseph E. Johnston. That fact slights the memory of one of the South's most trustworthy leaders. At one time or another Johnston held all of the major Confederate commands east of the Mississippi:

★ Army of the Shenandoah (1861)
★ Army of Northern Virginia (1861–1862)
★ Department of the West (1863)
★ Army of Tennessee (1863–1864)
★ Department of Tennessee and Georgia (1865)

Tourists who stroll Richmond's Monument Avenue see statues of Lee, Stonewall Jackson, and Jeb

General Joseph Eggleston Johnston

Stuart—but not Joe Johnston. Given a vote, the soldiers who fought for the South would have mended that error.

An event that took place in 1890 proves the point. That spring Johnston went to Atlanta for a reunion of the Army of Tennessee. As the procession formed, hundreds of veterans cheered and surged forward. Eager hands unhitched the horses from his carriage. Then the old soldiers bent to the task of pulling their hero along the parade route.[1]

Early Life

Joseph Eggleston Johnston was born in Farmville, Virginia, on February 3, 1807. He was the sixth son of a Revolutionary War veteran. Peter Johnston moved his family to a two-story log house in the mountain town of Abington in 1811. Young Joe learned to read and write at the Abington Academy. In his free time he hunted and fished in the nearby woods. Brown-eyed and brown-haired, he grew to a medium height of five feet seven inches. He looked frail, but he was tough enough to win an appointment to the United States Military Academy.

Johnston's strength of will showed clearly at West Point. He conquered night blindness and a weakness in math to graduate thirteenth in the forty-six-member Class of 1829. As a second lieutenant, Johnston saw combat in the Black Hawk War of 1832. He also fought the Seminoles in Florida in 1836. Anxious to make some money, he left the army in 1837 to work as a civil engineer. Jobs were scarce that year. When the army offered him a job in Florida as a surveyor, he took it. His coolness under fire during a Seminole ambush added to his reputation.

By mid-1838 Johnston was back in the army. Now a captain, he married Lydia McLane in 1845. They were a loving couple, but remained childless. When the Mexican War started in 1846, Johnston volunteered for combat duty. He took part in the siege of Veracruz and fought gallantly on the road to Mexico City. At Chapultepec Castle, Johnston braved heavy fire to plant the first flag on the ramparts. His gallantry earned him three promotions and an equal number of wounds.

Lieutenant Colonel Johnston spent the 1850s on the frontier. One of his jobs was to survey a route for a transcontinental railroad. Hard work and discipline were paying off. On June 28, 1860, Johnston was chosen the army's Quartermaster General.

The Civil War

Like many officers, Johnston had to make a choice when the Civil War began. His Northern friends urged him to stay in the United States Army. Johnston, however, felt duty-bound to defend his native state. He resigned his commission in April 1861 and boarded a train to Richmond. At his side was a prized possession—his father's Revolutionary War sword.

Johnston was fifty-four when he joined the Confederacy as a major general. In age and experience, he ranked fourth in the new army. His first post gave him a chance to show the defensive skills that marked his fighting style. Instead of staying at Harpers Ferry where he could be cut off, he moved to a stronger position at Winchester. His presence there kept Union forces from overrunning the rich Shenandoah Valley.

When the Union invaded Virginia in July, Johnston was called back to Richmond. He moved his troops by rail and arrived in time for the First Battle of Bull Run. As senior officer, he could have taken command. Instead, he chose to serve under General Pierre Beauregard, who knew the lay of the land. It was Johnston, though, who stepped forward at a crucial moment. The Northerners were about to break the left side of the line when he rallied his dazed troops. A seesaw battle turned into a major Southern victory.

In August the government gave Johnston the four stars of a full general. With the promotion came command of all Southern forces in northern Virginia. Unlike the South's politicians, the man his troops called "Old Joe" knew that the war was far from over. He shared his army's hardships and won its trust. The men liked this ramrod-straight general with the well-brushed appearance. On their behalf he begged for more soldiers, more guns, and more

As long as their men fought when called upon, Joe Johnston and his fellow generals turned a blind eye on scenes such as this. The three Southerners on the left have arranged a brief truce so they can trade tobacco for coffee.

supplies. The government wanted action, but Johnston would not be rushed.

A winter calm gave way to the spring fury of the 1862 Peninsula campaign. General George McClellan's Union army was advancing at last. Johnston fell back stage by stage, avoiding a full-scale battle. Shortening his lines reduced the danger of being outflanked. The cautious McClellan took months to move within striking distance of Richmond. In May, Johnston turned at last and hit McClellan's troops at Fair Oaks and Seven Pines. The fury of the Southern assault drove back the Bluecoats. At his moment of victory Johnston went down with wounds in his chest and thigh. With Johnston out of action, Robert E. Lee took command of the army.

Old Joe did not return to duty until fall. With Lee performing miracles in the east, President Jefferson Davis sent Johnston west. His new command was called the Department of the West. It was a general's nightmare—a badly divided command. Somehow Johnston had to control two armies—one in Tennessee and a second in Mississippi.

In May 1863, General U. S. Grant's Union army attacked Vicksburg. The South could not afford to lose the key river port. Johnston ordered General John Pemberton to attack Grant, but Pemberton refused. Next, as Grant closed in, Johnston ordered Pemberton to save his army by leaving Vicksburg. Pemberton again ignored the order. Johnston tried to go to his aid, but time ran out. Vicksburg fell on July 4.

Johnston's second problem general was Braxton Bragg. After Bragg lost a key battle at Missionary Ridge in November, Confederate President Davis accepted his resignation. Davis then swallowed his misgivings and turned the badly battered Army of Tennessee over to Johnston. In the weeks that followed, morale soared as the men responded to Old Joe's sure touch. Outnumbered two-to-one by General William Sherman's troops, Johnston slowly withdrew toward Atlanta.

Davis urged him to attack, but Johnston held back. His first goal was to keep his army intact, ready to pounce if Sherman made a mistake. His second goal was to keep the war dragging on. If he did so, war-weary Northern voters might elect someone less determined to preserve the Union than Abraham Lincoln. Given time, Johnston would have turned and fought on his own terms. On July 17, however, Davis replaced Old Joe with General John Hood. Hood did attack Sherman—and lost Atlanta in the process.

Six months later Lee gave Johnston another hopeless task. This time he was asked to stop Sherman's advance north through the Carolinas. His new army numbered only 30,000 men, and its units were scattered. Johnston pulled them together and won one last victory at Bentonville, North Carolina. The Bluecoats withdrew, then roared back stronger than ever. Johnston had no choice but to withdraw. A month later, on April 26, he surrendered to Sherman near Hillsboro, North Carolina.

Johnston's Legacy

Peacetime meant a return to civilian life. Johnston helped start an express company and served as president of a railroad. In 1868 a London insurance company hired him to run its offices in the deep South. By this time ex-Confederates were writing books that criticized Johnston's wartime conduct. In 1874, hoping to defend himself, he published his own book. It attracted few readers.

Johnston moved back to Richmond in 1876. A year later, at age seventy, he served a single term in Congress. Then, he spent six years traveling the country as the United States Commissioner of Railroads.

In 1891 Johnston went to the funeral of his old foe William Sherman. The New York weather was wet and cold. Urged to put his hat on, Johnston refused. "If I were in his place and he were standing in mine, he would not put on his hat," he snapped.[2]

Johnston paid for his gesture by catching a severe cold. The cold turned into pneumonia, and he died on March 21, 1891. A former soldier stepped forward to pay tribute in these words: "Farewell, old fellow! We privates loved you because you made us love ourselves."[3]

General Robert Edward Lee

Robert E. Lee
(1807–1870)

In April 1865 the Civil War was drawing to a close. General U. S. Grant's Union troops had cornered the remnants of General Robert E. Lee's Army of Northern Virginia. On April 9, Lee donned his best uniform and prepared to surrender. At the last moment General Edward Alexander proposed a plan to carry on the struggle. Alexander argued that the Confederate troops should take to the woods and conduct a guerrilla war. If Lee led the way, the men would follow.

Lee shook his head. "We must consider its effect on the country as a whole," he said. "Already it is demoralized by the four years of war. If I took your advice, the men would be . . . compelled to rob and steal in order to live. . . .[T]he enemy's cavalry would pursue them and overrun many wide sections they may never have occasion to visit. We would bring on a state of affairs it would take the country years to recover from."[1]

The point made, Lee rode out to meet Grant at Appomattox Court House. His calm acceptance of defeat saved the South from years of bloody guerrilla war.

Early Life

The South's best-loved hero was born January 19, 1807, at Stratford Hall, Virginia. His father, "Light Horse" Harry Lee, was a hero of the Revolutionary War. Six years after Robert's birth the family moved to a modest home in Alexandria, Virginia. The boy compiled a fine record at Washington Street School. One teacher noted, "He imparted a finish and a neatness, . . . to everything he undertook."[2] As a teenager, Lee nursed his ailing mother with the same care.

Lee wanted to go to college, but the family had little money. An 1825 appointment to the United States Military Academy solved the problem. At 18, Lee was tall at five feet eleven inches, erect, brown-eyed, and brown-haired. As a cadet, he made sure his work and conduct were nearly perfect. During four years at West Point, Lee did not receive a single demerit. He graduated second in the brilliant class of 1829.

The Army assigned Lieutenant Lee to the Corps of Engineers. While serving at Fort Monroe, Virginia, he courted Mary Custis, a relative of

Martha Washington. The couple married in 1831. Mary's health was poor, but over the years she gave Lee seven children. Lee loved his children dearly, but duty often kept him far from home.

In the late 1830s Lee designed and built river jetties that kept the port of St. Louis from silting up. A few years later he supervised work on the forts that guarded New York. The young officer saw combat for the first time during the Mexican War. In 1846 at Veracruz, Lee stormed ashore with General Winfield Scott's invasion force. On the road to Mexico City it was Lee who found a path through an "impassable" lava bed. Scott later called him "the very best soldier that I ever saw in the field."[3]

Promoted to colonel, Lee took charge of West Point from 1852 to 1855. His duties next took him to Texas, where he explored the frontier and picked sites for new forts. In 1859, while home on leave, Lee led the soldiers who captured the abolitionist John Brown at Harpers Ferry.

The Civil War

On April 12, 1861, the conflict between North and South flared into the Civil War. Four days later Virginia left the Union. President Lincoln sent a spokesman to ask Lee to take command of the Union army. Lee did not support secession and he disliked slavery. Even so, he would not draw his sword on his native state. Rather than take the offer, he resigned his commission.

Lee returned to Virginia, where he was given the rank of major general. When the state joined the Confederacy, he handed over control of his troops to the new government. At first Lee served as Confederate President Jefferson Davis's advisor. He could order troop movements, but other generals commanded the forces in the field.

When Union forces threatened western Virginia's rich Shenandoah Valley, Davis sent Lee to organize a defense. The campaign went badly, mostly because the local troop commanders refused to cooperate. Lee next moved south to plan construction of coastal forts. With the war going badly, Davis recalled him to Richmond early in 1862. Davis, in his role of Confederate Commander-in-Chief, kept control of the army. Lee's task was to carry out his decisions.

After General Joseph Johnston was wounded at Seven Pines, Lee took command of the Army of Northern Virginia. In early July he led his troops into a series of fierce battles called the Seven Days. Lee's soldiers, fighting with renewed confidence, repulsed the invading Northerners. The victory sent morale soaring.

Wherever Lee rode his iron-gray horse Traveller, men vowed to follow him—"even to hell." They knew that "Marse [Master] Robert" shared their hardships and dangers. As a general, he always seemed to be one move ahead of his opponents. Time after time he stung "those people" (he never called them Yankees) with fierce, well-planned counterattacks.

Lee thought one big victory on Northern soil might end the war. After winning the Second Battle of Bull Run, he invaded Maryland with fifty-five thousand men. When Lee's battle plans fell into Union hands, for once General McClellan moved quickly. The two armies met at Antietam in September 1862. Northern troops stopped Lee on that blood-soaked battlefield, but could not break his lines. Outnumbered and with his supply lines stretched thin, Lee had to retreat.

The Union soon returned to the offensive. On December 13, Lee's troops dug in to repel a frontal assault at Fredericksburg, Virginia. Confederate guns mowed down row after row of advancing Bluecoats. Lee turned to an aide as he stood watching the slaughter. "It is well that war is so terrible," he said, "or we should get too fond of it."[4]

Four months later Union forces were on the move again. Lee, ever a gambler, divided his outnumbered forces. The surprise move led to a Confederate victory at Chancellorsville on May 2, 1863. It was Stonewall Jackson, Lee's favorite general, who routed the Bluecoats. The victory was a costly one. Jackson died after mistakenly being shot by his own troops.

The war reached a turning point during Lee's 1863 thrust northward. The opposing armies met at Gettysburg, Pennsylvania, in a battle Lee would rather have postponed. On July 1 his men drove Union forces from the town, but failed to outflank them. On the second day a Confederate attack on the Union's southern flank was thrown back.

Still hoping for a breakthrough, Lee struck again on July 3. This time he ignored the advice of his staff and sent General George Pickett's division into the center of the Union line. Union guns atop Cemetery Ridge cut down the proud gray line. Lee soon knew that he had sacrificed brave men in vain. "All this has been my fault," he said. "It is I that have lost this fight."[5]

Lee's army was dwindling, but he was far from beaten. During 1864 he escaped traps set by General U. S. Grant—all the while inflicting heavy losses on his foes. Grant shook off the setbacks and pushed forward. By summer he had pinned Lee inside the Confederate defenses around Richmond and Petersburg. Southern soldiers were short of almost everything. Men marched and fought barefoot.

On April 1, 1865, Grant's troops broke through Lee's defenses near Five Forks. As Union columns advanced unchecked, Lee sent word that Richmond should be evacuated. His hungry army straggled westward toward the Blue Ridge Mountains. Hopes of escape vanished when a Union column seized a food train Lee had counted on. April 8 found the Confederate army at Appomattox Court House, sixty miles from Richmond. The encircling Union forces outnumbered Lee's men five to one.

Lee sat down and wrote to Grant, "I now ask an interview."[6] On April 9, convinced that further fighting was useless, Marse Robert surrendered.

Fighting a defensive war meant digging in. General Robert E. Lee's troops quickly became experts at building strong fortifications. Barriers such as those pictured here effectively stalled Union forces at Vicksburg, Atlanta, and Richmond, for months at a time.

Lee's Legacy

Lee's surrender signaled the collapse of the Confederacy. Now it was time to turn to the tasks of peace. Lee's estate at Arlington had fallen into federal hands (and would become a national cemetery). Nearing sixty, nearly broke, and slowed by heart trouble, Lee needed a job.

Washington College in Lexington asked Lee to serve as its president. At the time the school had only five teachers and a handful of students. Lee moved into the president's house and gathered his family around him. Under his leadership, enrollment grew and donations rolled in. In place of Greek and Latin, he emphasized science, technology, and modern languages.

Summers spent at White Sulphur Springs could not repair Lee's ailing heart. In September 1870 he suffered a stroke and soon developed pneumonia. Doctors could do little for him. Lee died on October 12. Legend says that his last words were "Strike the tent."[7]

Robert E. Lee set high standards of himself—and lived up to them. In 1868 he scolded some young Southerners who had snubbed a Northern guest. "I believe I may say," he told them, "looking into my own heart, and speaking as in the presence of my God, that I have never known one moment of bitterness or resentment."[8]

James Longstreet
(1821–1904)

In December 1862 the Union army was advancing through northern Virginia. Ahead lay the Southern capital at Richmond. On December 13, Federal troops threw a pontoon bridge across the Rappahannock River at Fredericksburg. After a sharp fight the Southerners abandoned the town. Columns of Bluecoats moved forward with orders to storm the heights above the town. Ahead lay a broad plain, a sunken road, and a stone wall.

General James Longstreet's troops waited behind the stone wall. Longstreet asked his artillery captain if he had enough firepower. The officer laughed. Not even a chicken could survive out there, he promised.[1]

The Southerners opened fire when the Bluecoats were a hundred yards away. Longstreet watched as his

General James Longstreet

riflemen fired and stepped back to reload. Instantly, a new line replaced them, rifles at the ready. The deadly curtain of fire chopped the first Union wave to bits. More blue-clad waves formed and swept forward. Each met the same fate. At last the Union general called off the assault. He had lost 7,300 men to Longstreet's 1,450 casualties.

No one who saw the slaughter ever forgot it. A defensive stand, Longstreet realized, evened the odds against a stronger foe. From that day on, he tried to turn each battle into another Fredericksburg.

Early Life

James Longstreet was born January 8, 1821, in Edgefield, South Carolina. He was the fifth of eleven children. The family moved to Augusta, Georgia, where his father died when James was twelve. By then the boy had spent three years in his uncle's private school. He loved to ride, hunt, and read books on great battles. No one was surprised when he chose an army career.

Appointments to the United States Military Academy were rationed, a few going to each state. Longstreet had to move to Alabama to find an opening. He entered West Point in 1842, and excelled in drill and horsemanship. Bookwork held little interest for him, a fact proven by his grades. He ranked fifty-fourth in a class of fifty-six cadets.

At six feet two inches tall and 200 pounds, with piercing blue-gray eyes and a high forehead,

Longstreet stood out in a crowd. His fellow cadets voted him the "most handsome" man in the class. He had little to say, perhaps because he was slightly deaf.

In 1846 Lieutenant Longstreet reported for duty at Jefferson Barracks, Missouri. While serving there, a distant cousin named Julia Dent became engaged to a fellow officer, Ulysses S. Grant. The outbreak of the Mexican War in 1846 sent Longstreet into combat in northern Mexico. He later fought under General Winfield Scott in central Mexico. In two years of warfare he fought in eight battles and was wounded at Chapultepec.

Longstreet came home from the war to marry Maria Louise Garland. The army then assigned him to a post on the Texas frontier. To help support his growing family, he took on the extra-pay duty of paymaster. When the Civil War broke out in 1861, Major James Longstreet's heart lay with the South. He resigned his commission and put on a Confederate uniform.

The Civil War

Longstreet asked for a post as a supply officer, but the Confederate army needed his combat skills. After being sworn in, the new brigadier general was sent to Manassas, Virginia. On July 18, his Fourth Virginians drew first blood in a brief skirmish with Union troops. Three days later, in the First Battle of Bull Run, he showed the coolness under fire that became his trademark. Sword in hand, "Old Pete" rode into heavy fire to rally some men who had panicked. The trust he inspired in his men helped him earn the rank of major general in October.

Three months later scarlet fever raged through Richmond. Called home by his wife, Longstreet found three of his ten children dead or dying. Already a man of few words, he now drew deeper into himself. His staff had to be content with little more than "yes" or "no" responses.

In 1862 Longstreet helped repel a second Union thrust into Virginia. His division fought at Yorktown, Williamsburg, and in the bloody Seven Days' battles outside Richmond. Longstreet led the cheers when the South put up its only hot-air observation balloon. The women of Richmond had sacrificed their silk dresses to make it possible. By that time General Robert E. Lee had taken command of the Army of Northern Virginia. Lee praised Longstreet, calling him "my old war-horse."[2]

In August, Longstreet delivered a crushing counterattack at Second Bull Run. His success led him to argue that Lee's plan to invade the North was flawed. Longstreet lost the debate, but fought brilliantly at Antietam in September. If Longstreet's line had broken that day, Lee's army would have been cut in two. A month later Lee promoted Old Pete to the rank of lieutenant general.

During a campaign Lee often traveled with Longstreet's corps. The two men had forged an almost brotherly bond. Even so, they often argued

Like his fellow generals on both sides, James Longstreet welcomed information obtained by observers who went aloft in observation balloons. The North, with its superior technology, used hydrogen generators to inflate its balloons. The South countered with a single hot-air balloon made from silk dresses contributed by the women of Richmond.

over tactics. Lee longed to carry the war into the North. Longstreet wanted to fight a defensive war. Longstreet's critics charged that Lee was keeping an eye on his slow-moving corps commander. Rock solid on defense, Old Pete sometimes took too long to deliver an attack. His victory at Fredericksburg in December further convinced him that defense would win the war.

In May 1863 Longstreet missed the Battle of Chancellorsville. Lee had sent him south to gather supplies and block a Union advance along the coast. In June he was at Lee's side when the Confederate army marched north. The invasion ground to a halt at Gettysburg in early July. After two days of fighting ended in stalemate, Lee ordered a frontal assault. Longstreet was dead set against the risky move. In later years he wrote that he "went to Lee's headquarters at daylight and renewed my views against making an attack."[3]

Lee gambled that his battle-tested troops could carry the day. On July 3 he told Longstreet to send General George Pickett's division against the Union forces on Cemetery Ridge. Once again Longstreet was slow in moving to the attack. It was 4:00 when Pickett led 15,000 men forward in a splendid charge. As Longstreet had feared, the assault was beaten back with heavy losses. Later, critics blamed the defeat on Longstreet's footdragging. At the time, Lee told his men, "I alone am to blame."[4]

In the west, Confederate forces were reeling backward. In September, Lee sent Longstreet with two divisions to support General Braxton Bragg. His troops reached Georgia in time to fight at Chickamauga. Longstreet poured men into a gap in the Union lines and sent the Northerners reeling from the field. Like the other Southern generals, he was outraged when Bragg did not pursue the beaten Bluecoats. Bragg then sent the angry Longstreet off to attack Knoxville. Longstreet took a week to ready his assault, a delay the Union troops used well. When the attack came, the Confederates could not crack the improved defenses.

By April 1864 Longstreet was back with Lee. General U. S. Grant had invaded Virginia with a massive army. In May, Lee struck Grant's forces in a tangle of woods known as the Wilderness. On the second day, Old Pete's men turned the tide with an all-out counterattack. Longstreet was riding through tangled smoky woods when his column collided with a second Southern force. In the confusion, both groups opened fire. A bullet smashed through the general's neck and right shoulder. His staff officers were in tears as they put him in an ambulance.

Longstreet returned to duty in October, his right arm dangling at his side. He tried to cover Lee's flanks during the siege of Richmond, but it was a futile effort. The Confederates were outgunned and outfought. In April 1865 Old Pete commanded the rear guard during the retreat from Richmond. A few days later, Lee surrendered at Appomattox.

Longstreet's Legacy

After the war Longstreet made his home in New Orleans. A practical man, he now joined the ruling Republican party. The harsh laws of the Reconstruction era were the price of losing the war, he argued. Old Pete paid a stiff price for appearing to side with the North. His friends melted away and his cotton business failed.

U. S. Grant kept in touch with his old friend. After he became president, Grant named Longstreet to a post as surveyor of customs. That job led to later positions as postmaster, tax collector, and United States marshal. In 1880 Old Pete served briefly as minister to the Ottoman Empire (now Turkey).

Longstreet was not the only former officer to take a job with the federal government. Because he had held high rank, and because he was the first, some Southerners called him a traitor. A few of his old comrades also attacked his war record. Longstreet wrote his memoirs as a way of defending himself. His book *From Manassas to Appomattox* was published in 1896.

Perhaps Longstreet had the last laugh. He outlived most of his critics and was spry enough in 1897 to remarry. A year later President William McKinley named him a United States Railway Commissioner. It was Old Pete's last post. He died at age eighty-two on January 2, 1904.

General George Edward Pickett

George Edward Pickett
(1825–1875)

General George Edward Pickett left his mark on history at Gettysburg, Pennsylvania, on July 3, 1863. For two days, the armies of the North and the South had been locked in the Civil War's greatest battle. Now the Confederate army gathered its strength for one final assault.

For two hours, cannon fire pounded the Union troops on Cemetery Ridge. When the firing stopped, Pickett began the assault that General Robert E. Lee had ordered. His division of fifteen thousand determined soldiers marched forward as though on parade. The Union lines lay half a mile away, across grassy open fields.

Pickett did not know that the artillery barrage had overshot its targets. The Northern soldiers held their fire as the gray lines moved closer. Then with a shattering roar the Union guns opened up. Shells ripped huge gaps in Pickett's formations. The Confederates did not waver. As men died, their mates closed ranks and pressed onward. Now they were close to the Union lines. The men screamed the high-pitched Confederate yell and scrambled forward through heavy rifle fire. A few hundred Southerners broke through, only to be shot or captured. The rest of the attackers turned and stumbled back to their own lines.

A dazed Pickett found Lee waiting for him. "General Pickett," Lee said, "place your division in the rear of this hill, and be ready to repel the advance of the enemy."

Head bowed, Pickett replied, "General Lee, I have no division."[1]

Early Life

The colorful general who led Pickett's Charge was born on January 28, 1825, in Richmond, Virginia. Young George grew up on his father's plantation. Of medium height, he was good-natured, friendly, and fearless. He dressed in ruffled shirts, and scented his long curly hair with cologne. Despite his love of fine clothes and scent, he chose the army as a career.

Pickett entered the United States Military Academy in 1842. His love of frills soon clashed with West Point dress codes. Each infraction cost him another demerit. He almost flunked out, but held on to graduate in 1846. In a class of fifty-one cadets, he ranked fifty-first.

The outbreak of the Mexican War gave Pickett his first taste of combat. He fought with General Winfield Scott at the siege of Veracruz. From day one he displayed courage under fire. He was wounded at Buena Vista and took part in the capture of Mexico City. During the war, promotions came quickly. By September 1847 he had risen to captain. In a private tragedy, his first wife died ten months after their marriage.

In 1855 Pickett was transferred to the Pacific Northwest. The United States was caught in a dispute with Great Britain over some islands in Puget Sound. Backed by sixty soldiers, Pickett occupied San Juan Island. The British answered by sending three warships filled with combat-ready marines. Pickett stood his ground. "I shall order my men to fire," he said, "if a man of them lands on this island."[2] A British admiral stepped in to prevent a shooting war. In time diplomats settled the dispute peacefully.

During his stay in the northwest, Pickett spent time with the local American Indians. They taught him their language and customs. To repay their friendship, he translated songs and prayers for their church services. All this time, war clouds were gathering back home.

The Civil War

The Civil War was three months old when Captain George Pickett resigned from the United States Army. After crossing the continent he joined the Confederate army as a major of artillery. Four weeks later he was a colonel, assigned to defend Virginia's lower Rappahannock region. He plunged into his duties with a zest that earned him the rank of brigadier general in February 1862. As a brigade commander, he served under one of his heroes, General James Longstreet.

The war entered a new phase with the Union invasion of Virginia in 1862. Pickett won praise for the way he handled his brigade at Williamsburg and Seven Pines. In June, at the battle of Gaines's Mill, a Union bullet smashed his shoulder. The wound kept him out of action until fall.

When he returned, the elegant Pickett carried the rank of major general. He now commanded a division that included four Virginia brigades. In December, Pickett's men held the center of the Southern line at Fredericksburg. It was a key spot, but the Union attack hit another one of Longstreet's divisions. The glory that day fell to the riflemen dug in on the slopes of Marye's Heights.

Pickett saw little action during the months that followed. He and his men were fresh and eager when they arrived at Gettysburg in July 1863. If Longstreet had planned the battle, Pickett's Charge would never have taken place. Old Pete tried to convince Lee that the attack on Cemetery Ridge was risky at best. Lee saw the danger but believed his troops could overcome the odds.

Pickett, sensing a new chance for glory, welcomed the chance to lead the assault. When the moment came, he called out to his soldiers, "Up, men, and to your posts! Don't forget today that you are from Old Virginia."[3] Then he led his perfect battle line forward. A Union officer described the scene: "Right on they move, as with one soul, in perfect order, . . . over ridge and slope, through orchard and meadow, and cornfield, magnificent, grim, irresistible." Moments later the Union guns tore the fine gray ranks to shreds.

Pickett's place in the army was never the same after Gettysburg. The feeling spread that the dapper Virginian was not fit to manage a division. One officer noted that Longstreet "always . . . looked after Pickett, and made us [explain] things very fully [to him]; indeed, sometimes stay with him to make sure he did not get astray."[4]

Like the South's fortunes, Pickett's life veered up and down. A high point was his marriage to young Sallie Corbell on September 15, 1863. It was his vow to Sallie that had kept him from drinking and gambling. A low point was his division's stay in North Carolina. Sent there to rebuild, Pickett attacked Union forces at New Bern in January 1864. The assault failed because of poor planning and worse

The story of Pickett's Charge at Gettysburg lives on in the history books. This haunting image of a dead Confederate sharpshooter reminds us that the Virginians paid a heavy price for putting on that brave show. This photo was taken at a site called Devil's Den on the Gettysburg battlefield.

execution. A furor arose when Pickett ordered the hanging of twenty-two deserters. He explained that the men deserved their fate. They had been captured wearing Union uniforms.

Pickett marched his division north to rejoin Longstreet's First Corps in June 1864. During the siege of Richmond, his troops manned defense lines near Petersburg. In those long, dull days that followed, Pickett let his command fall into wretched shape. Day after day he badgered Longstreet for leave to visit his new bride. If he was refused, he sneaked off to Richmond anyway. In January 1865, Lee warned Longstreet that the problems in Pickett's division had to be fixed.

In March, Lee assigned Pickett to defend the army's last escape route "at all hazards." On March 31, Pickett's troops turned back a Union cavalry thrust near Five Forks. The next day, confident that the Bluecoats would not attack, Pickett went off to a fish fry. When the surprise attack came, he ran a gauntlet of rifle fire to reach his command post. By then his line was broken and the battle was lost.

On April 8 an angry Lee relieved Pickett of his command. Told to report to Confederate President Jefferson Davis, Pickett stayed with the army. He was at Appomattox when Lee surrendered a day later.

Pickett's Legacy

President Abraham Lincoln visited Richmond on April 4. One of his stops was at the home of Sallie and George Pickett. Lincoln had not forgotten that he had once helped George make it into West Point. Told that his friend was with the Confederate army, Lincoln hugged Pickett's baby son. He told the child, "Tell your father, the rascal, that I forgive him for the sake of your bright eyes."[5]

Lincoln's death on April 14 sent shock waves through the South. Pickett fled to Canada, fearful that he would be arrested. When he returned, he took a job with an insurance company. His wartime fame brought an offer to serve as a general in the Egyptian army. President U. S. Grant offered to appoint him to a post as a United States marshal. Pickett turned down both jobs.

Even though Lincoln and Grant forgave him, Lee did not. Lee argued that Pickett's carelessness led to the defeat at Five Forks. Pickett was just as bitter. Speaking of Lee, he said, "That old man . . . had my division massacred at Gettysburg."[6]

Pickett stayed on better terms with his corps commander. "I am now an old man," he wrote to Longstreet in 1872. "It looks to me but Yesterday . . . I first delivered you a dispatch at Centerville."[7] He was not yet fifty, but his health was failing. He died of liver disease on July 30, 1875.

In America's memory, George Pickett still leads his gallant soldiers forward. Pickett's Charge shines brightly in the nation's long history of wartime valor and sacrifice.

"Jeb" Stuart
(1833–1864)

On October 13, 1863, General "Jeb" Stuart was out hunting Bluecoats. Near Auburn, Virginia, he halted his cavalry brigades at the top of a hill. On the plain below lay thousands of Union wagons. Stuart longed to attack, but there were too many Northerners in the area. Moments later his scouts reported that a second force was coming up behind them. The hunters had stumbled into a trap.

Stuart quickly concealed his troops in a small wooded valley. Union soldiers set up a camp just 150 yards away. When night fell, Stuart dispatched riders to tell General Robert E. Lee what had happened. An officer proposed that they escape by breaking through the Union line. Stuart refused. The plan might work, but it meant leaving his cannon behind.

General James Ewell Brown Stuart

At first light the nearest Union troops began to cook breakfast. An hour later, Stuart and his men heard rifle fire. It was Lee's foot soldiers coming to the rescue. Stuart's gunners did their part by firing on the Union camp. The surprise attack scattered the Northern units. The cavalrymen mounted and rode to safety behind their daring leader.

Early Life

James Ewell Brown Stuart—Jeb for short—was born February 6, 1833, in a Virginia farmhouse. He was the seventh child in a family of eleven children. Jeb grew up to be a tall gangly youth who was happiest when he was on horseback. At age twelve he promised his mother he would never drink liquor. He kept that pledge, even in the final painful moments of his life.

Most of Jeb's early schooling took place at home. As a teenager he attended Emory and Henry College. In 1850 he received an appointment to the United States Military Academy. By then he had grown to five feet ten inches in height, with reddish hair and blue eyes. His classmates called him "Beauty," a joking tribute to his strong plain features. He was fun-loving and full of pranks, but he earned good marks at West Point. On graduation day in 1854 he ranked thirteenth in his class.

The army sent the new lieutenant to Texas to serve with the Mounted Rifles. From day one, he showed an utter lack of fear in battle. His reward was a posting to the crack First Cavalry at Fort Leavenworth, Kansas. Fighting the Cheyenne taught him how to lead a cavalry force. In his free time he courted pretty Flora Cooke. She became his wife in 1855.

In 1859 Stuart took Flora east to meet his family. He also used the trip to show two inventions to army officials. One was a quick release hitch for horses. The other was a device for hanging a saber from a trooper's belt. While Stuart was in Washington, John Brown attacked Harpers Ferry. When Colonel Robert E. Lee headed out with a detachment of marines, Stuart went along as his aide. At Harpers Ferry, it was Stuart who conferred with Brown and who signaled for the final assault.

Stuart returned to Kansas, but the Civil War was about to change everything. When the Southern states seceded, men had to choose to stay or go. Flora's father chose to fight for the Union. Jeb Stuart resigned his commission on May 4, 1861, and headed south.

The Civil War

On May 9 the Confederate army assigned Stuart to an infantry regiment as a lieutenant colonel. At Harpers Ferry he reported to Colonel Thomas (soon to be Stonewall) Jackson. Jackson put Stuart where he would do the most good—in the cavalry. In July, Stuart rose to full colonel and took command of the First Virginia Cavalry. As the month ended, the unit earned the respect of the army at the First Battle of Bull Run. Stuart led a cavalry charge that shattered a Union regiment and helped save the day.

In the weeks that followed, Stuart set up cavalry outposts across northern Virginia. One forward post stood within sight of Washington. The army took note of Stuart's brilliance and promoted him to brigadier general. General Joe Johnston wrote, "He is a rare man, wonderfully endowed by nature with the qualities necessary for an officer of light cavalry. Calm, firm, acute, active, and enterprising."[1] His men were delighted to hear him sing in a rich, clear voice as he rode into battle. Soon they were singing one of his favorite songs:

> *If you want a good time,*
> *Jine [join] the cavalry; jine the cavalry!*[2]

Stuart's fame skyrocketed during the 1862 Peninsula Campaign. As General George McClellan's Union forces neared Richmond, Lee sent the cavalry to scout the advance. Stuart quickly turned the mission into a wild adventure. In four days, from June 12 to 15, he led twelve hundred troopers on a 100-mile "ride around McClellan" that circled the Union army. Along the way the Confederates burned a million dollars worth of Union supplies. Stuart slowed from time to time to kiss (and be kissed by) admiring Southern women. On the last leg he rode forty-eight hours straight to carry his reports to Lee.

Stuart's ride helped pave the way for Lee's offensive late in June. In the battles known as the Seven Days, the cavalry scouted Union movements and led infantry attacks. Stuart's troopers inflicted their greatest damage behind Northern lines. They cut telegraph wires, tore up railroad tracks, and seized supply wagons. At one point Union forces burned a big supply depot to keep Stuart from seizing it. Lee rewarded his heroic cavalry officer by promoting him to major general.

Major General Stuart led the South's most daring cavalry force. At times he seemed to turn war into a game. Stuart still sang as he led his troopers into battle, an ostrich plume waving from his cap. At night, around the campfire, he ordered banjo players to strike up lively dance tunes. During one raid, he paused to send a telegram to President Lincoln. "The last draw of wagons I've just made are very good," he complained, "but the mules are inferior stock, scarcely able to haul off the empty wagons. . . . I've had to burn several valuable wagons before getting them in my lines."[3]

In the spring of 1863 Stuart's scouting reports allowed Lee to go on the attack. The Southern victory at Chancellorsville, however, was dimmed by the death of Stonewall Jackson. It was Stuart who stepped forward to take command of Jackson's corps. On May 2, he led two charges that drove Union troops from the field. Stuart wanted to keep the command, but Lee sent him back to the cavalry. The army counted on Stuart to screen Confederate troops, scout Union movements, and raid supply lines.

In June, Lee crossed into Maryland and Pennsylvania. Stuart's task was to swing northeast to link up with General Jubal Early's troops. In the days that followed, Stuart stretched his orders to the limit. He ranged far afield and ripped Union supply lines, but sent no reports. As a result Lee stumbled into a battle at Gettysburg that he had not planned. When Stuart arrived on the second day, Lee sent for him. "I have not heard a word from you for days," Lee scolded, "and you [are] the eyes and ears of my army."[4] After Pickett's Charge failed on July 3, Stuart covered Lee's retreat back to Virginia.

On May 11, 1864, Union and Confederate cavalry clashed at Yellow Tavern, Virginia. Stuart, his reddish beard gleaming in the sun, plunged into the thick of the battle. He had been shot at many times, but his luck was about to run out. A Union private fired point-blank as the Confederate officer dashed by. Stuart pressed a hand to his side. "I'm afraid they've killed me," he told one of his officers.[5] An ambulance rumbled across sixty miles of rutted roads to carry the wounded man to Richmond. True to his pledge, Stuart turned down the whiskey that might have dulled the pain. Doctors did what they could, but the great cavalryman died the next day.

A Civil War artist captured the drama of a Union cavalry charge at Brandy Station in June 1863. Almost hidden by the onrushing Northerners, Jeb Stuart's troopers have formed a defensive line to give their slow-moving artillery time to escape. Both sides suffered heavy losses in the swift-moving engagement.

Stuart's Legacy

Historians still debate the importance of Stuart's absence during Lee's advance on Gettysburg. Critics charge him with playing a major role in the South's defeat. His defenders note that Lee himself said that Stuart's orders gave him freedom of movement. General Jubal Early added that Stuart's cavalry could not have added any more data than did the army's own scouts.

More to the point, Lee did not lose faith in the man he thought of almost as a son. "[Stuart] never brought me a piece of false information," he said.[6]

Stuart's men remembered him fondly. "He never showed a sign of fatigue," one of his officers noted. "He led almost everything. Even after he became a general officer, . . . I frequently followed him as my leader in a little party of half a dozen troopers."[7] His men added, "Jeb never says, 'Go, boys,' but always, 'Come, boys.'"[8]

Jeb Stuart himself may have had the last word. "All I ask of fate is that I may be killed leading a cavalry charge," he once said.[9] The gods of war must have been listening.

Military Units

During the Civil War, the North and the South organized their fighting forces, according to a model in which progressively larger units were assigned increasing responsibilities. An order that originated at headquarters in Washington, D.C., or in Richmond, Virginia, would flow (➜) step-by-step through this chain of command:

UNIT	DESCRIPTION
Army ↓	A combat and administrative unit assigned to a particular department of war. An army generally consists of a headquarters, two or more fighting corps, and the necessary support forces. *Commander*: a four-star general or a lieutenant general.
Corps ↓	A combat unit composed of two or more infantry divisions, plus artillery, cavalry, and support troops. *Commander*: a lieutenant general.
Division ↓	A combat unit (6,000 to 9,000 soldiers) made up of two or more brigades, self-contained and equipped for prolonged fighting. *Commander*: a major general.
Brigade ↓	A combat unit composed of a headquarters unit, two or more regiments of infantry, plus artillery, cavalry, and support units. *Commander*: a brigadier general or colonel.
Regiment ↓	A combat unit (1,000 or more soldiers) made up of at least two battalions. *Commander*: a colonel.
Battalion ↓	A combat unit consisting of a headquarters company and four or more infantry companies, artillery batteries, or similar units. *Commander*: a lieutenant colonel or a major.
Company ↓	A tactical or administrative unit (approximately thirty soldiers), made up of two or more platoons. *Commander*: a captain or a first lieutenant.
Platoon	The army's smallest tactical unit, composed of about twelve soldiers. *Commander*: a second lieutenant, assisted by a sergeant.

The Officer Corps

Armies depend on a corps of commissioned officers to guide and direct all phases of military operations. Success or failure often hinges on the skill, courage, and dedication of officers up and down the chain of command. Newly commissioned officers usually begin service as second lieutenants. Here's the path that leads upward from there, along with the insignia for each rank:

CATEGORY	RANK, INSIGNIA, and COMMAND RESPONSIBILITY
Line Officers *(Also called company grade officers or junior officers)*	Second lieutenants (gold bar)—assistant platoon commanders First lieutenants (silver bar)—platoon commanders and assistant company commanders Captains (two silver bars)—company commanders
Field Grade Officers *(Also called senior officers)*	Majors (gold oak leaf)—assistant battalion commanders Lieutenant colonels (silver oak leaf)—battalion commanders Colonels (silver eagle)—regiment and assistant brigade commanders
General Officers *(Confederate generals all wore three stars enclosed by an oak wreath.)*	Brigadier generals (one star)—brigade commanders Major generals (two stars)—division commanders Lieutenant generals (three stars)—corps and army commanders Generals (four stars)—army commanders

Note: In the hurly-burly of the Civil War, both sides assigned command responsibilities as dictated by circumstances. When officers of the proper rank were unavailable, lower-ranking officers often stepped in to take command of units their training and experience had not prepared them to lead. Both governments also made political appointments, some of which awarded high rank to men who were poorly qualified to lead soldiers into battle.

Glossary

abolitionist—Someone who worked to abolish slavery in the years before the Civil War.

ambush—A sudden or surprise attack made from a concealed position.

artillery—An army unit made up of cannons, their gunners, and transport for moving the guns.

assault—A large-scale attack launched against an enemy position.

barrage—A sustained period of artillery fire directed against enemy positions.

casualties—Military personnel killed, wounded, or missing in battle.

cavalry—In the 1800s, a highly mobile army unit trained to fight from horseback.

charge—A fast determined assault against an enemy position.

Confederacy—The union of southern states that fought for independence from the United States during the Civil War.

counterattack—A return assault made in response to an earlier enemy attack.

department—A geographic region, organized to support military operations.

deserters—Military personnel who leave their units without authorization.

dragoons—Heavily armed, mounted soldiers—i.e., cavalry troopers.

drill—The repetitious exercises used to train recruits to march in formation and use their weapons.

engineers—Military units trained to construct fortifications, bridges, railroads, and roads.

field hospital—A medical unit set up near a battlefield to care for casualties.

flank—The left or right side of a military unit's formation.

forts—Fortified defensive positions set up to defend important towns, cities, ports, and farmlands.

frontier—A thinly populated area on the edge of a settled region.

gallantry—Heroic behavior in battle. Armies recognize gallantry by awarding medals.

guerrillas—Fast-moving armed bands that operate outside the normal laws of warfare.

infantry—Combat units trained to fight on foot.

offensive—A military maneuver designed to advance into enemy territory.

outflank—A tactic that puts troops in position to attack an enemy's vulnerable flanks.

outpost—An outlying military post, usually held by a small number of troops.

parole—An agreement that releases a prisoner of war, based on the prisoner's promise not to fight again.

pontoon bridge—A temporary floating structure that allows troops to cross a river.

quartermaster—The officer in charge of supplying food, clothing, and equipment to a military unit.

rangers—During the Civil War, soldiers trained to patrol and defend an area, usually from horseback.

rear guard—Troops sent to slow or stop an enemy advance, thus giving their own army a chance to retreat.

recruits—Volunteers and draftees who must be trained before they can be sent into battle.

retreat—The process of pulling back from a fortified position.

secession—The act of withdrawing from a political alliance.

sentry—A soldier or sailor who stands guard at an assigned position.

shrapnel—Deadly chunks of metal hurled through the air by an exploding shell.

siege—A prolonged attack that traps defenders within a fortified position.

skirmish—A small-scale clash between forward units of opposing armies.

stockade—A defensive wall made of poles set upright in the ground.

strategy—A military plan calculated to win a battle, campaign, or war.

supply line—The route over which supplies move to an army at the front.

tactics—The maneuvers an army uses to carry out its strategy.

troopers—A term often applied to soldiers who ride with a cavalry unit.

truce—An agreement to suspend fighting while peace talks go on.

Union—The states that remained loyal to the federal government during the Civil War.

wagon train—Transport vehicles used by an army to carry ammunition, food, supplies, and casualties.

wings—The units assigned to the left and right sides of an army's position in the field.

Chapter Notes

Chapter 1

1. Brian Steel Wills, *A Battle from the Start: The Life of Nathan Bedford Forrest* (New York: HarperCollins Publishers, 1992), p. 12.

2. Curt Anders, *Fighting Confederates* (New York: G. P. Putnam's Sons, 1968), p. 123.

3. Jack Hurst, *Nathan Bedford Forrest: A Biography* (New York: Alfred A. Knopf, 1993), p. 94.

4. J. Harvey Mathes, *General Forrest* (New York: D. Appleton & Co., 1902), p. 155.

5. Jeffrey Ward, *The Civil War: An Illustrated History* (New York: Alfred A. Knopf, 1990), p. 335.

6. Mark M. Boatner III, *The Civil War Dictionary* (New York: David Mackay, 1962), p. 289.

7. B. A. Botkin, ed., *A Civil War Treasury of Tales, Legends and Folklore* (New York: Random House, 1960), p. 184–185.

Chapter 2

1. Nathaniel C. Hughes, Jr., *General William J. Hardee, Old Reliable* (Baton Rouge: Louisiana State University Press, 1965), p. 288.

2. William D. Pickett, *Sketch of the Military Career of William J. Hardee* (Lexington, Ky.: James E. Hughes, 1910), pp. 3–4.

3. Hughes, p. 80.

4. Ibid., p. 115.

5. Ibid., p. 313.

Chapter 3

1. Douglas Southall Freeman, *Lee's Lieutenants: A Study in Command, Vol. I* (New York: Charles Scribner's Sons, 1942), p. 189.

2. Ibid., p. 663.

3. Martin Schenck, *Up Came Hill* (Harrisburg, Pa.: The Stackpole Co., 1958), p. 333.

4. William W. Hassler, *A. P. Hill* (Richmond, Va.: Garrett & Massie, 1957), p. 2.

5. Schenck, p. 334.

Chapter 4

1. Robert Leckie, *None Died in Vain; The Saga of the American Civil War* (New York: HarperCollins Publishers, 1990), p. 607.

2. John Dyer, *The Gallant Hood* (New York: Bobbs-Merrill Co., 1950), p. 88.

3. Colonel Red Reeder, *The Southern Generals* (New York: Duell, Sloan and Pearce, 1965), p. 105.

4. Frank E. Vandiver, *Their Tattered Flags: The Epic of the Confederacy* (New York: Harper & Row, 1970), p. 279.

Chapter 5

1. Robert Leckie, *None Died in Vain; The Saga of the American Civil War* (New York: HarperCollins Publishers, 1990), p. 167.

2. B. A. Botkin, ed., *A Civil War Treasury of Tales, Legends and Folklore* (New York: Random House, 1960), p. 211.

3. John Bowers, *Stonewall Jackson, Portrait of a Soldier* (New York: William Morrow & Co., 1989), p. 314.

4. Frank E. Vandiver, *Their Tattered Flags: The Epic of the Confederacy* (New York: Harper & Row, 1970), p. 202.

5. Leckie, p. 460.

6. Botkin, p. 205.

Chapter 6

1. Craig L. Symonds, *Joseph E. Johnston: A Civil War Biography* (New York: W. W. Norton & Co., 1992), p. 380.
2. Ibid., p. 380.
3. Ibid., p. 381.

Chapter 7

1. Frank E. Vandiver, *Their Tattered Flags: The Epic of the Confederacy* (New York: Harper & Row, 1970), pp. 303–304.
2. Curt Anders, *Fighting Confederates* (New York: G. P. Putnam's Sons, 1968), p. 238.
3. Patrick Austin Tracey, *Military Leaders of the Civil War* (New York: Facts on File, 1993), p. 5.
4. B. A. Botkin, ed., *A Civil War Treasury of Tales, Legends and Folklore* (New York: Random House, 1960), p. 203.
5. Philip Van Doren Stern, *Robert. E. Lee* (New York: McGraw Hill, 1963), p. 182.
6. Fitzhugh Lee, *General Lee* (New York: DeCapo Press, 1994), p. 392.
7. Stern, p. 244.
8. Emory M. Thomas, *Robert E. Lee* (New York: W. W. Norton & Co., 1995), p. 392.

Chapter 8

1. Bruce Catton, *Never Call Retreat* (Garden City, N.Y.: Doubleday & Co., 1965), p. 18.
2. Gamaliel Bradford, *Confederate Portraits* (Freeport, N.Y.: Books for Libraries Press, 1914), p. 70.
3. Fitzhugh Lee, *General Lee* (New York: De Capo Press, 1994), p. 277.
4. Colonel Red Reeder, *The Southern Generals* (New York: Duell, Sloan and Pearce, 1965), p. 142.

Chapter 9

1. George R. Stewart, *Pickett's Charge* (Boston: Houghton Mifflin Co., 1959), p. 256.

2. Walton Rawls, *Great Civil War Leaders and Their Battles* (New York: Abbeville Press, 1985), p. 271.

3. Douglas Southall Freeman, *Lee's Lieutenants: A Study in Command, Vol. III* (New York: Charles Scribner's Sons, 1942), p. 157.

4. William C. Davis, *The Confederate General, Vol. 5* (National Historical Society, 1991), p. 34.

5. B. A. Botkin, ed., *A Civil War Treasury of Tales, Legends and Folklore* (New York: Random House, 1960), pp. 511–512.

6. John C. Waugh, *The Class of 1846* (New York: Warner Books, 1994), p. 529.

7. Davis, p. 34.

Chapter 10

1. William C. Davis, *The Confederate General, Vol. 6* (National Historical Society, 1991), p. 19.

2. B. A. Botkin, ed., *A Civil War Treasury of Tales, Legends and Folklore* (New York: Random House, 1960), p. 217.

3. Ibid., p. 221.

4. Burke Davis, *Jeb Stuart: The Last Cavalier* (New York: Rinehart Company, 1957), p. 334.

5. Ibid., p. 408.

6. Ibid., p. 419.

7. Botkin, pp. 25-26.

8. Glenn Tucker, *Lee and Longstreet at Gettysburg* (Indianapolis: Bobbs-Merrill Co., 1968), p. 203.

9. Ibid.

Index

A

Alexander, Gen. Edward (CSA), 67

Anaconda Plan, 5

Antietam (Md.), Battle of, 31–32, 34, 54, 71, 79

Appomattox Court House, 68, 72, 91

Army of Northern Virginia, 57, 67, 70, 79

Atlanta (Ga.), Battle of, 19, 27, 39, 46, 59, 64

B

Beauregard, Gen. Pierre (CSA), 35, 61

Bee, Gen. Barnard (CSA), 50

Black Hawk War, 59

Bragg, Gen. Braxton (CSA), 17, 26–27, 64, 82

Brown, John, 69, 96

Bull Run (Va.), First Battle of, 25, 35, 49–50, 61, 78–79, 97

Bull Run (Va.), Second Battle of, 36, 54, 71, 79

C

Chancellorsville (Va.), Battle of, 36, 38, 71, 81, 98

Chattanooga (Tenn.), Battle of, 27

Chickamauga (Ga.), Battle of, 17, 43, 45, 82

D

Davis, Pres. Jefferson (CSA), 38, 39, 41, 45, 63, 64, 70

E

Early, Gen. Jubal (CSA), 55, 101

Ewell, Gen. Richard (CSA), 56

F

Five Forks (Va.), Battle of, 91

Forrest, Gen. Nathan Bedford (CSA), 12–20

Fort Donelson, 16

Fort Pillow, Battle of, 17, 19

Fort Sumter, Battle of, 4

Franklin (Tenn.), Battle of, 19, 39, 46

Fredericksburg (Va.), Battle of, 36, 43, 45, 54, 71, 75, 77, 88

G

Gaines's Mill (Va.), Battle of, 43, 52, 88

Gettysburg (Pa.), Battle of, 37, 43, 45, 56, 71–72, 81, 85–86, 88-90, 99

Grant, Gen. U. S. (USA), 26, 37, 63, 67, 72, 78, 82, 83, 92

H

Hardee, Gen. William Joseph (CSA), 21–29

Harpers Ferry (W. Va.), 51, 54, 61, 69, 96

Hill, Gen. Ambrose Powell (CSA), 30-38

Hood, Gen. John Bell (CSA), 19, 39–47, 64

Hooker, Gen. Joseph (USA), 55

J

Jackson, Gen. Thomas "Stonewall" (CSA), 33, 35, 36, 38, 43, 48-56, 71, 96
Johnston, Gen. Albert Sidney (CSA), 26
Johnston, Gen. Joe (CSA), 21, 27, 35, 57-65, 70, 97

K

Ku Klux Klan, 20

L

Lee, Gen. Robert E. (CSA), 31, 36, 37–38, 42, 43, 47, 52, 54, 56, 63, 66-74, 79, 81, 86, 91, 92, 96, 98, 99, 101
Lincoln, Pres. Abraham (USA), 64, 69, 91–92, 98
Little Sorrel, 49, 55
Longstreet, Gen. James (CSA), 43, 45, 75–83, 88–89, 92

M

McClellan, Gen. George (USA), 31–32, 33, 52, 63, 71, 97
Mexican War, 24, 32-33, 51, 60, 69, 78, 87
Murfreesboro (Tenn.), Battle of, 17, 20, 26

N

Nashville (Tenn.), Battle of, 19, 41, 46

O

Observation balloons, 79–80

P

Pemberton, Gen. John (CSA), 63-64
Petersburg (Va.), Siege of, 37, 72, 91
Pickett, Gen. George (CSA), 72, 81, 84–92
Pickett's Charge, 85–86, 92

Pope, Gen. John (USA), 54

R

Reconstruction, 20, 83
Richmond (Va.), 5, 37, 38, 42, 51, 57, 70, 72, 79, 82, 91
"Ride around McClellan," 97

S

San Juan Island, 87
Savannah (Ga.), Battle of, 21, 27
Scott, Gen. Winfield (USA), 5, 69, 78, 87
Seminole War, 23, 33, 51, 59
Seven Days, Battle of the, 36, 70, 79, 98
Shenandoah Valley Campaign, 52, 70
Sherman, Gen. William (USA), 21, 39, 46, 64–65
Shiloh (Tenn.), Battle of, 13, 16, 26
Stuart, Gen. "Jeb" (CSA), 93–101

T

Taylor, Gen. Zachary (USA), 24
Thomas, Gen. George (USA), 41
Traveller, 70

U

U.S. Military Academy (West Point, N.Y.), 6, 23, 24, 32, 41–42, 50, 59, 68, 69, 77, 86, 95

V

Vicksburg (Miss.), Battle of, 63–64
Virginia Military Institute, 51

W

Washington College, 74
Wilderness, Battle of the, 82